BUSINESS PLANNING IN LOCAL GOVERNMENT

John Delderfield IEng, FIWHM, MIMBM, MInstWM, MBIM Deputy Director, City Services, Cambridge

Ray Puffitt MA, DMS, DMA Lecturer, INLOGOV

Graham Watts AILAM Director, City Services, Cambridge

BUSINESS PLANNING IN LOCAL GOVERNMENT

Published by Longman Industry and Public Service Management,
Longman Group UK Ltd, Westgate House, The High,
Harlow, Essex CM20 1YR, UK
Tel: (0279) 442601
Fax: (0279) 444501

First published 1991
First reprint 1991
Second reprint 1991

A catalogue record for this book is available from the British Library.

ISBN 0-582-08198-X

Designed and typeset by City Services, Cambridge (0223) 358977
Printed in Great Britain by Page Bros. Norwich

FOREWORD

The 1980s was probably the most dramatic era that local government has ever faced. Within that turbulent decade the rule book was completely rewritten, and for one group of officers at least, entirely new disciplines had to be learnt.

Those of us charged with the responsibility of managing direct labour organisations which were required by law to make a profit, found that we needed to carry out pioneering exercises in our efforts to succeed. It is true that there was useful advice available in the shape of the legislation and the CIPFA accounting code of practice, but beyond that we were very much on our own.

The need to prepare our organisation for competition meant that we had many difficult and protracted problems to resolve, frequently working in isolation. The concept of business planning was as remote as political unity. Ten years on, it looks as though the disciplines of competition are not only here to stay, but will be extended to many more aspects of local government within the foreseeable future.

However, most of the pioneering may now be over, for the publication of "Business Planning in Local Government" will provide managers with a process designed to deal with the many problems which competition bring. The authors have used their combined commercial skills and local government experience to produce a book which should prove an essential addition to the repertoire of knowledge of every senior officer in all local authorities in the UK.

The Association of Contract Services Chief Officers is delighted to recommend the book to both Members and Officers alike for its clear understanding of local government generally, and its detailed analysis and examination of the process of business planning, which is increasingly needed in the local government environment.

Jim Patterson
National Chairman
Association of Contract Services Chief Officers

Dartford
April 1991

ACKNOWLEDGEMENTS

We are deeply indebted to and have drawn heavily upon the pioneering ideas of John Argenti in his book "Corporate Planning", first published in 1968. This book applied the concept of "Corporate Planning" strictly to private sector enterprises and unhappily had little influence on the movement toward corporate planning in local authorities in the early 1970s.

With the emerging interest in the application of Business Planning to the work of local authorities, the ideas in his book have taken on a new significance and we have endeavoured to take forward these ideas and translate and remould them into the political setting in which local authorities operate. Any errors in such translation and remoulding are entirely our own. Similarly, the work of Michael Porter on "How Competitive Forces Shape Strategy", have influenced and modelled our own consideration of the environmental factors which bear upon a local authority undertaking.

Our thanks are also due to Tony Bovaird of the University of Aston Business School for permission to use an illustration of an hierarchy of objectives taken from his paper on "Performance Measures in Leisure Services" and to Ann Brown of Cranfield Business School from whom we have gained inspiration and ideas in the joint seminar work we have undertaken on behalf of the School of Public Policy at the University of Birmingham.

We would like to record our thanks to Lawrie Weaver and Eddie Hewett of Cambridge City Council for their contributions to the work undertaken in the practical applications set out in Part II. Thanks are also due to Althea Mejias of Cambridge City Council for undertaking the unenviable task of typing the original manuscripts from our own illegible handwriting.

Finally we wish to record our very deep appreciation of the work of Janet Wilson of Cambridge City Council for her reformulation and reproduction of our basic work into the much clearer format here presented.

Cambridge
April, 1991

CONTENTS

GLOSSARY OF TERMS USED

INTEGRATION BACKWARD: A strategy to secure control over the source of supplies.

INTEGRATION FORWARD: A strategy to secure control over the demand for a service.

MEANS: Those actions which an organisation will take only if they improve the ability to reach objectives or targets.

PLAN: A list of actions so ordered as to achieve an objective or target.

PRIMARY OBJECTIVE: It is an objective which is fundamental to the nature of the authority and is relatively permanent.

It may well be that an objective which the local authority has accepted may yet be regarded by an individual department as a RESTRAINT (see definition of RESTRAINT) and which they may feel it is necessary to challenge.

(Officers often suggest that the manifesto promises of a majority political party are also primary objectives. Naturally, it would be imprudent for a senior officer not to prepare a contingency plan as to what actions might be taken to achieve such promises, but they cannot be regarded as primary or even secondary objectives until they have received Council approval).

RESTRAINTS: Those actions which an organisation will take on moral or political grounds **whether or not** they improve the ability to reach objectives or targets.

(Argenti uses the terms CONSTRAINTS but we find that this term in practical usage in local authorities is often used to describe what is no more than an organisational weakness or an environmental threat. Accordingly, we much prefer the term RESTRAINT because it implies the self-imposition of boundaries and parameters within which the authority intends to operate).

SECONDARY OBJECTIVES: Those objectives which, though not Primary Objectives themselves, lead towards the achievement of a Primary Objective (see page 4 for an hierarchy of objectives).

TARGET: An objective expressed in numerical, quantifiable or action terms.

BIBLIOGRAPHY

"Corporate Planning", John Argenti *(Allen and Unwin)*

"The 24 Hour Business Plan", Ron Johnson *(Hutchinson Business Books)*

"The Business Plan Work Book", C. & P. Barrow *(Kogan Page)*

"Business Planning", Business Support Group *(Institute of Chartered Accountants)*

"Performance Measurement in Leisure Services", Tony Bovaird *(Aston Business School)*

"The Marketing Plan", MacDonald and Morris *(Heineman)*

PART I

THE PROCESS

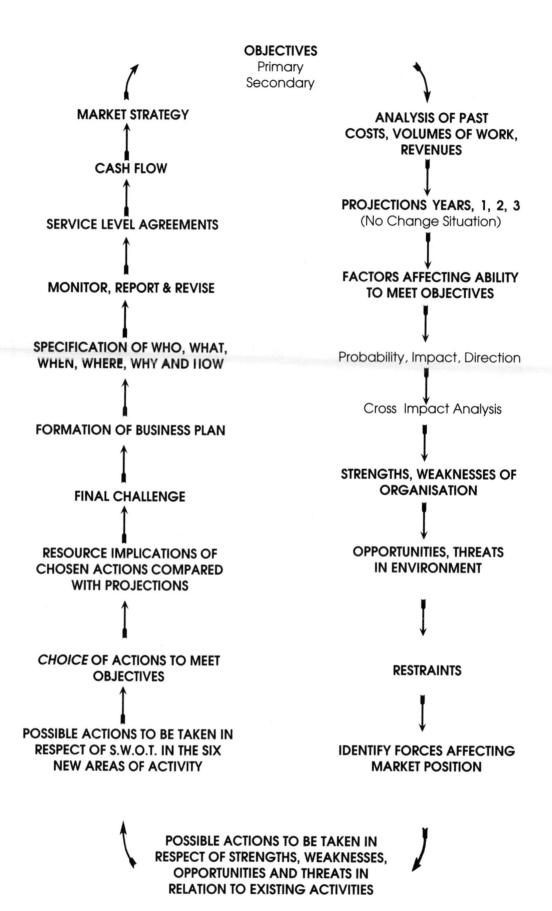

OBJECTIVES
Primary
Secondary

MARKET STRATEGY

CASH FLOW

SERVICE LEVEL AGREEMENTS

MONITOR, REPORT & REVISE

SPECIFICATION OF WHO, WHAT, WHEN, WHERE, WHY AND HOW

FORMATION OF BUSINESS PLAN

FINAL CHALLENGE

RESOURCE IMPLICATIONS OF CHOSEN ACTIONS COMPARED WITH PROJECTIONS

CHOICE **OF ACTIONS TO MEET OBJECTIVES**

POSSIBLE ACTIONS TO BE TAKEN IN RESPECT OF S.W.O.T. IN THE SIX NEW AREAS OF ACTIVITY

ANALYSIS OF PAST COSTS, VOLUMES OF WORK, REVENUES

PROJECTIONS YEARS, 1, 2, 3
(No Change Situation)

FACTORS AFFECTING ABILITY TO MEET OBJECTIVES

Probability, Impact, Direction

Cross Impact Analysis

STRENGTHS, WEAKNESSES OF ORGANISATION

OPPORTUNITIES, THREATS IN ENVIRONMENT

RESTRAINTS

IDENTIFY FORCES AFFECTING MARKET POSITION

POSSIBLE ACTIONS TO BE TAKEN IN RESPECT OF STRENGTHS, WEAKNESSES, OPPORTUNITIES AND THREATS IN RELATION TO EXISTING ACTIVITIES

BUSINESS PLANNING IN LOCAL GOVERNMENT

1. INTRODUCTION

From where does the notion arise that local authorities and their departments should produce Business Plans?

On the face of it, the idea is almost a contradiction in terms. Traditionally, local government has been viewed as a mechanism whereby the rights and interests of people in a locality could best be protected; where each local issue and problem could be given full discussion so as to obtain a clear understanding; where legitimate and peaceable expression of local views could take place; where innovation and experimentation with solutions to local problems was encouraged; where opportunity was provided for political education and where a bulwark against the arbitrary use of central power existed.

How then does the idea that local government should produce Business Plans fit into this traditional view of the virtues of local self-government?

The answer is that the idea of Business Plans emerges from a totally different view of local government - a view that stems jointly from the work of W. Niskanen on Representative Government, and G. Tullock on Voting Motives. Both of these works represent criticisms of public bureaucracies.

Niskanen argues that the market place is the best allocator of resources for it maximises choice. Local government, not being part of the market place, must therefore be inherently flawed.

Tullock, argues that electoral checks are too weak in public bureaucracies, that elected members are by nature vote-grabbing and officers budget-maximising. In essence, that **producer** interests are always dominant.

The answer to this problem from their respective positions is to create a market-place of the public sector, to break up monopolies of provision and to generate internal markets within bureaucracies. It is this strand of thought that underpins the legislative, financial and political changes which have been taking place in local government over the last few years. In turn, it is from this background of change that many local authorities, encouraged by bodies like the Audit Commission, CIPFA and LGTB, are now seeking to produce Business Plans, not merely for their direct labour departments, but for the authority as a whole and for all their respective departments.

It is inevitable, therefore, that trying to apply ideas drawn from a solely private sector arena into the world of the local authority must create problems of translation.

We have tried in this document to outline a process of thinking and analysis which will enable a local authority or any constituent department to produce a Business Plan to guide its affairs, but which takes account of the traditional values of local self-government. In particular, that the over-riding concern of a local authority is to bring benefit to the community it serves.

Formal literature about producing a Business Plan is somewhat sparse. Moreover, where it exists it is usually specifically directed towards acquiring financial resources.

"The Business Plan is a ticket of admission to the investment process"
(P.D Carman).

Clearly, this is a definition far removed from the requirements of a local authority department or a DSO, where Business Plans will have a very different purpose.

A more useful, though short, definition in the context of a local authority organisation, is that the Business Plan is,

"A list of ACTIONS so ordered as to attain the desired OBJECTIVES derived from a careful analysis of the FACTORS likely to affect the organisation".

It should provide a clear guide to the overall strategy and the ACTIONS the organisation will take over a determined time period to manage the THREATS and OPPORTUNITIES it will face. It will be a guide to what elected members and clients may expect of the organisation and the actions to be taken by elected members, management and the supporting workforce.

> **"WHAT CAN THE PROCESS OF PRODUCING A BUSINESS PLAN ADD TO ORGANISATIONS THAT MIGHT ALREADY FEEL OVER BURDENED BY PLANNING SYSTEMS?"**

This is a question which might legitimately be asked of an institution that has already been through four types of planning mechanism since the middle 1960s (Planning Programme Budgetting Systems, Management by Objectives, Corporate Planning and various statutory or non-statutory departmental planning mechanisms).

The answer lies in the definition which we have adopted; namely, that it emphasises the ACTIONS that an organisation is going to take. It is specific about what it intends to do. Furthermore, it is a planning process that in many ways can be built up from the bottom of the organisation in that it is the individual departments and indeed even the individual business centres where the initiative for producing the Business Plans will lie.

Assuming that the present intention of the Government to reorganise local government is carried through, then for those authorities such as district councils who may obtain new functions, the result will in many ways be analogous to a private sector organisation which has decided both to **diversify** its interests and to **integrate forward** at the same time. These terms are explained more fully at the start of Chapter 7. The **diversification** will arise from the receiving authority taking on a range of activities of which it has no recent previous experience and the **integration forward** arising from some departments of the authority gaining a greater measure of influence over the demand for the services they provide.

Receiving authorities and departments will therefore be in the position of being able to utilise the concept of a Business Plan, both to implement the run-up to the acquisition of new functions and for a re-examination, from their own perspective of any Business Plans which have been formulated for those services which are to be received.

Clearly, the Business Plans of departments and business centres will have to reflect the overall strategic objectives of the local authority but the initiative and ownership of Business Plans will rest with the sub-units of the authority and its departments. They will differ considerably from, for example, a Mission Statement for the Business Plan is more an analytic tool than a motivational one.

Nevertheless, in a local authority organisation it must contain the overall values that derive from the purpose of the local authority.

In private sector organisations the fundamental underlying purpose, the raison d'être, is to make a profit. Often, when talking to private sector managers, they will assert a series of what are really only sub-objectives (eg. to gain a larger share of the market). But this is exactly what it is - a sub-objective. It will not, nor cannot, be pursued unless in the long-run it will contribute to the profitability of the organisation.

For local authorities generally, the fundamental underlying purpose will not be so easy to define. For DSO's, however, the purpose is at its clearest, because the DSO is currently statutorily required to make a surplus or to break-even in the case of building cleaning and leisure management. This clear commercial objective may be in conflict with political, public service and even managerial objectives.

One purpose of the local authority Business Plan is therefore to show to elected members, senior officers, the workforce and the ultimate consumers of the service, how a particular department within a local authority intends to reconcile these conflicting interests. Accordingly, we believe that the VALUE STATEMENTS derived in part from the Mission Statement of the authority are an essential part of the Business Plan for they give guidance to staff as to how conflicting interests should be reconciled.

Values are derived from the overall purpose or ultimate objectives of a department but the problem with objectives in a local authority setting is that they are often bland, generalised, ambiguous and sometimes inconsistent with one another. For the purpose of a Business Plan they need to be "sharpened" so that staff can ask themselves, "How has my activity contributed to the objectives of the department or to assessed change in those objectives?" Accordingly, such objectives need to be specifiable in some way and ordered into a hierarchy of objectives which in effect become an essential part of the production process of the organisation or department. Performance indicators can then be attached to each level of objectives. An example is shown in the diagram overleaf.

Given that a primary objective of the local authority is to reduce accidents in the water, then sub-objectives contribute to this - through changes in awareness of danger, levels of physical hazard, attitudes of the public towards risk and level of skills in dealing with dangerous situations. Clearly, each of these second level objectives can in turn be broken down into lower level objectives.

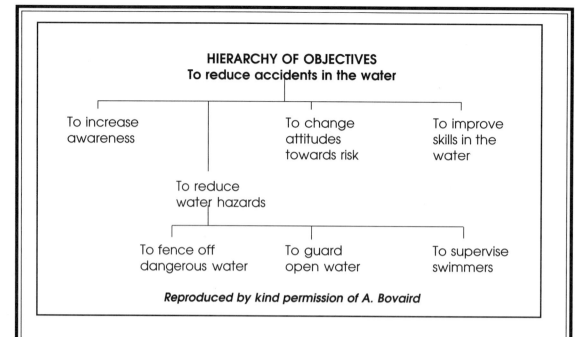

HIERARCHY OF OBJECTIVES
To reduce accidents in the water

| To increase awareness | To change attitudes towards risk | To improve skills in the water |

To reduce water hazards

| To fence off dangerous water | To guard open water | To supervise swimmers |

Reproduced by kind permission of A. Bovaird

The key advantages of this approach are that, because:

- the cause-and-effect relationships between objectives can be spelt out

- the level of performance of lower level objectives can be established, even when performance of the top level objectives is hard to measure

- there is an opportunity to test whether changing performance against primary objectives is truly related to achievement of lower level objectives (especially important when the primary objectives are affected by many more factors than the authority's intervention)

priority objectives can clearly be indicated and the logical need for whole **pathways** of objectives to be seen as priorities is highlighted.

In considering the process of Business Planning as applied to local government, we have been aware of the wide range of authorities, in terms of both political direction and size and diversity of functions. There are some councils who see themselves as "enabling authorities" and, with political commitment to this end, are striving to apply the Business Planning concept to the definition of the objectives and action plans of the corporate or client role.

On the other hand, there are authorities who are just as committed to the provision of efficient and effective in-house services on merit. Business Planning for them is an essential tool for achieving this aim. Whilst we do not propound either or any other specific course of action, we have generally based our work on the latter scenario, but believe that the process set out in the following chapters is capable of interpretation in all or any forms of local government organisation.

2. Agreeing and Clarifying Objectives

How then might a local authority and its departments begin to clarify and get agreement about its objectives?

We have hinted earlier that the PRIMARY objective of a local authority and a department is something FUNDAMENTAL to the nature of the authority and the department and which distinguishes it from other types of organisation. It is something that is relatively permanent and not merely a current fashion or whim.

If the organisation failed to achieve the PRIMARY objective, it would prejudice the continued existence of the organisation or at least would bring about significant proposals for its abolition or fundamental change.

There are therefore, three test questions one can ask of on objective which is proposed as a primary objective for a local authority or a department.

> **1.   Under what circumstances would the authority/ department NOT TRY to achieve such objectives?** -
>
> The expected answer must be - *"None"*
>
> **2.   Why does the authority/department wish to achieve this particular objective?**
>
> The expected answer must be - *"In order to survive or withstand fundamental criticism"*
>
> **3.   If the authority/department failed to achieve the proposed objective would it also fail as an authority/ department or prejudice its continued existence?**
>
> The expected answer must be - *"Yes"*

Local authorities and their departments usually have multiple objectives. Indeed, we have seen many Business Plans from local authorities which provide a long list of so-called KEY OBJECTIVES often with no priorities attached to them. On examination they are often found to be mutually inconsistent in that to vigorously pursue one objective would make it difficult or impossible to pursue another.

This is evidence of a list of alleged key objectives that in reality are a mixture of PRIMARY OBJECTIVES (in that they meet the required answers from the above test questions), SECONDARY OBJECTIVES which lead toward the attainment of PRIMARY OBJECTIVES and the RESTRAINTS which the organisation has chosen to impose upon itself.

The following analysis might suggest that we are taking a rather restrictive view of the role of local authorities. This view flows not from the analysis but from the fact that local authorities are creatures of statute. They do not yet have a power of general competence. Accordingly the analysis produces PRIMARY OBJECTIVES which are statements or close extensions of the mandatory statutory functions allocated to local authorities. In reality, it is the SECONDARY OBJECTIVES which the local authority itself has chosen as the MEANS to achieving its PRIMARY OBJECTIVES which for many authorities will be given prominence in their Business Plans.

Let use now try out these three test questions against some of the objectives which local authorities set for themselves. We propose a list that is a mixture of DSO objectives and those of a more generally applicable nature.

SUGGESTED OBJECTIVES

1   To increase our share of the market for a particular service
     (eg grounds maintenance)

2   To increase the volume of a service provided
     (eg housing repairs)

3   To lead the local government field in an area of activity
     (eg equal opportunities training for DSO staff).

4   To increase production of an activity (eg manufacture of
     uPVC windows)

5   To be a good employer

6   To meet an obligatory statutory requirement (eg meet the
     rate of return)

SUGGESTED OBJECTIVE 1 - (SHARE OF MARKET)

Question 1 Under what circumstances would the local authority NOT TRY to increase its share of the market? (eg grounds maintenance)

> *Expected answer* - None

> *Actual answer* - If to do so would prejudice its ability to secure its rate of return

Question 2 Why does the local authority wish to increase its market share for grounds maintenance?

> *Expected answer* - In order to survive or withstand fundamental criticism

> *Actual answer* - In order to secure its rate of return

Question 3 If the local authority failed to increase its market share for grounds maintenance would it also fail as a local authority?

> *Expected answer* - Yes

Actual answer - No, as long as it was securing its rate of return on other work undertaken

The suggested objective has failed all three test questions. To increase the local authority's share of a market is not the local authority's primary objective or even the primary objective of a sub-unit such as the DSO grounds maintenance business centre.

The second listed objective "To increase the volume of a service provided (eg. housing repairs)" will receive the same set of replies from the test questions and again is not a primary objective even of a business centre. They could, however, both be important SECONDARY OBJECTIVES leading to the attainment of a PRIMARY OBJECTIVE.

SUGGESTED OBJECTIVE 3 - (TO LEAD THE LOCAL GOVERNMENT FIELD IN AN AREA OF ACTIVITY)

The third question will now be put through the same test questions to identify whether or not it could be a PRIMARY OBJECTIVE.

Question 1 Under what circumstances would the local authority or its DSO NOT TRY to lead the local authority field in an area of activity? (eg equal opportunities training for DSO staff)

> *Expected answer* - None

> *Actual answer* - In any situation where it impaired the ability of the local authority to meet obligatory statutory objectives or in the case of the DSO if it impaired its ability to secure its rate of return

Question 2 Why does the local authority want to lead the field in a particular activity? (eg equal opportunities training for DSO staff)

> *Expected answer* - In order to survive or withstand fundamental criticism

> *Actual answer* - To improve its standing with other local authorities, its elected members, its employees and its customers

Question 3 If the local authority failed to lead the local government field in an area of activity (eg. equal opportunities training for DSO staff) would it also fail as a local authority or prejudice its continued existence?

> *Expected answer* - Yes

> *Actual answer* - Not necessarily - indeed very unlikely

Suggested Objective 3 "To lead the local government field in an area of activity" is clearly revealed as not being a PRIMARY OBJECTIVE for it has failed our three questions. Similarly, Suggested Objective No 4 "To increase production of an activity" if put to the test would fail all three questions. It may, however, be a possible SECONDARY OBJECTIVE.

SUGGESTED OBJECTIVE 5 - (TO BE A GOOD EMPLOYER)

Now, let us test out Suggested Objective No 5 - an objective much stated by local authorities and their departments.

Question 1 Under what circumstances would the local authority or a constituent department (eg a DSO) NOT TRY to be a good employer?

Expected answer - None

Actual answer - None

Question 2 Why does the Local Authority or a constituent department (eg DSO) want to be a good employer?

Expected answer - In order to survive or withstand fundamental criticism

Actual answer(s) - Because it is a proper thing to do;

Because in the long-run it might increase our ability to meet other objectives or our rate of return;

Because it keeps the Personnel Officer and the Trade Unions happy

Question 3 If the local authority or a constituent department (eg DSO) failed to be a good employer would it also fail as a local authority or prejudice its continued existence?

Expected answer - Yes

Actual answer - Unlikely

Again, this suggested objective failed the test - for it failed two questions out of three. But it differs in kind from the other objectives in the following way.

Under no circumstances would the local authority NOT TRY to be a good employer - that is to say that on moral or political grounds the local authority would wish to be a good employer and that even if it could be proved that by being a bad employer it could actually *increase* its ability to meet its statutory obligatory objectives (eg a required rate of return) it would not wish to do so. This is a critically important point for local authorities because many of the objectives they set for themselves are not PRIMARY OBJECTIVES in the Business Planning sense. They may be moral or political objectives but in reality they can often be RESTRAINTS upon achieving PRIMARY OBJECTIVES.

> **RESTRAINTS** are those Actions which a Local Authority will take on moral or political grounds <u>whether or not</u> they improve the ability to reach **PRIMARY** objectives.

SUGGESTED OBJECTIVE 6 - (TO MEET AN OBLIGATORY STATUTORY REQUIREMENT)

This now brings us to our final Suggested Objective.

Question 1 Under what circumstances would a local authority NOT TRY to meet an obligatory statutory requirement? (eg to meet the rate of return)

> *Expected answer* - None

> *Actual answer* - None - unless it had political motives in not so doing

Question 2 Why does the local authority wish to meet an obligatory statutory requirement? (eg the required rate of return)

> *Expected answer* - In order to survive or withstand fundamental criticism

> *Actual answer* - In order to survive or withstand fundamental criticism.

Question 3 If the local authority failed to meet an obligatory statutory requirement (eg the required rate of return) would it fail as a local authority (or as a DSO)?

> *Expected answer* - Yes

> *Actual answer* - Yes, otherwise there would be little point in that obligatory statutory requirement being allocated to local authorities

Suggested Objective No 6 has passed the three test questions and is clearly therefore a PRIMARY OBJECTIVE.

In this analysis we in no way wish to challenge how local authorities perceive themselves in their relationship with the community - only to assist in sorting out the difference between PRIMARY OBJECTIVES, the MEANS by which PRIMARY OBJECTIVES might be achieved and the RESTRAINTS which the local authority is prepared to impose upon itself just because it is a public sector body and is prepared to take on board ethical, moral and political considerations. It is only by the careful thinking through of exactly what are the PRIMARY OBJECTIVES, what are the MEANS by which they are to be achieved and the RESTRAINTS the authority is prepared to work under, that a situation can be reached whereby RESTRAINTS can be seen for what they are and be challenged if needs be, and that MEANS can be modified to accomplish objectives.

The central purpose of the analysis is to ensure that elected members, management, staff, clients and the electorate can see how the multitude of conflicting interests that appear to exist in a local authority and its departments can be resolved.

The Business Plan(s) are route-maps to what the local authority wishes to achieve, the ACTIONS it is going to take and the moral and political considerations which will guide it.

WORK TO BE DONE
(Clarifying Objectives)

1   Identify (from policy papers, minute books, manifestos etc) what are the stated objectives for your authority/department

2   Subject such objectives to the "three-question" test

3   Identify a primary objective

4   Determine the sub-objectives and create a hierarchy of objectives

5   Identify initially which suggested objectives are in reality

    (i)   MEANS to achieving objectives
       (note them for later use)

    (ii)   RESTRAINTS upon achieving objectives
       (note them for possible later challenge)

6   Discussion with elected members and staff as to their views upon the OBJECTIVES and RESTRAINTS identified

7   Gain agreement on/modification of your initial hierarchy of objectives

8   Discussion with the staff and trades unions represented in the department to gain agreement on the OBJECTIVES, MEANS and RESTRAINTS

NB Once the process of preparing a Business Plan is under way new objectives will emerge, new means of meeting these objectives will be voiced and greater clarity regarding the restraints will develop.

In certain instances, it will also be possible to discusss objectives, means and constraints with the client or the client's representative. Certainly, where one department is the client of the other this should be possible depending upon relationships. Even where the client is in a way external to the department, then discussions may still be possible. For example in a Social Services Department, with the need to produce a care plan for each individual requiring care, there exists the possibility of discussing such issues with carer groups.

3. ANALYSIS OF THE PAST

For a completely new business or undertaking, the starting point for a Business Plan might well be the analysis of the market place, but for a local authority which is in effect an on-going business, we have made the CLARIFICATION AND AGREEMENT OF OBJECTIVES our point of commencement. Moreover, an on-going business has the advantage of a history which can be probed to produce rich information for the Business Plan.

In essence, this involves identifying what has happened in the past (say over the last 3-5 years) in respect of the volume of work/activity undertaken, the costs associated with such activity and the revenues (sometimes proxy revenues) which have been produced or could have been produced.

VOLUMES OF WORK/ACTIVITY

Depending upon the precise nature of the department, hopefully information will be available on such matters, as for example:

- The hours of policy advice provided

- The time spent in detailed administration

- The number of activities undertaken eg school meals provided, inspections carried out etc.

- The square metres achieved (eg cleaning, paving)

- The hours spent in care or counselling of a client

- The time taken in consultaton/negotiation, meetings etc

- The volume of salt spread on a regular round

- The number and type of plumbing emergencies carried out

- The volumes of refuse collected

- The numbers and types of users of a swimming pool

We know that there is often some difficulty for local authorities in producing such information, but with the move toward the establishment of service specifications, many authorities now have much more detailed data on the activities and volumes of work produced by their staff. We see this as essential in identifying what work output might be expected from a given mix of resources. Without this data, even in crude form, it becomes exceedingly difficult to predict what extra level of work activity can legitimately be expected from additional increments of resource.

For example, how can you know with accuracy how many additional painting staff, training staff or legal staff to employ to meet increased demands for a particular type of activity?

Some local authority Business Plans we have examined are somewhat skimpy on this type of information or omit it entirely. The assertions made and the exhortations for more resources can seem to be based solely on acts of faith, rather than data or evidence.

WORK TO BE DONE
(Analysis of the past)

1   What are the measures of work output/activity you would deem appropriate for the work of your department and its business centres?

2   How should this be measured?

3   What might the "norm" performance be?

4   How has work output changed over time?

5   Is this resource-related, ie more resources = more work activity?

COSTS - (OF EXISTING AND HISTORICAL LEVELS OF ACTIVITY)

When examining the past, we need to consider costs. We have had many discussions with the representatives of Treasurers departments about what categories are useful in this type of analysis and whether such data can be made available.

The sadness is that in many local authority departments the financial information which would be invaluable in identifying trends and anomalies, and making valid projections as to what costs might look like in the future, is not readily available in a useful form. At a very basic level, the sort of costs we would wish to identify and understand would be:

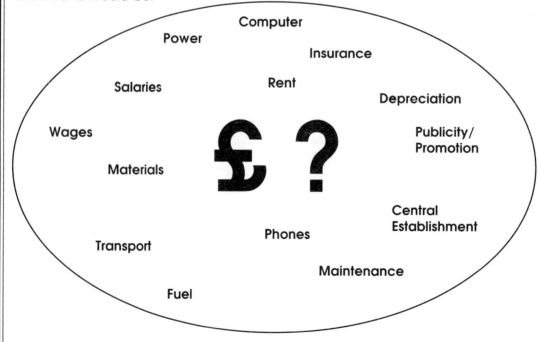

Data on such items would seem crucial if a Business Plan was to have a solid base.

Given such data one could begin to analyse whether any anomalies existed eg, were salaries over a given time period growing in greater proportion than wages.

There may well be valid reasons for such an occurrence but at least the data would have alerted us to ask the question.

Perhaps, for example transport costs have suddenly begun to rise - why should this be? Is it validated by extra work activity being undertaken or is it due to some other cause? Naturally, every item of cost could be examined in this way, though we have to say it is the major items of expenditure which would require our closest scrutiny. Explanation is one reason for such scrutiny, but also if we wished to carry out a FUNCTION/COST ANALYSIS exercise, whereby we sought to provide the same function/activity at a lower cost, this data and exploration would be necessary.

At the very least, analysis of such cost items gives a better understanding of what is driving the costs of a department and the inter-relationships which inevitably exist between one cost and another.

We would also wish to explore what part of each cost was fixed or relatively fixed and did not vary with output, and those which were VARIABLE with output. We accept the point of view of the economists that no fixed cost is fixed for ever etc, but nonetheless the exploration of what are the fixed and variable costs alerts us to changing situations that may affect our output. One does not have to prepare one's PROJECTIONS with minute accuracy and to try to do so would waste an inordinate amount of time.

This is not to say that we should restrict our analysis to only the past three years. If data is available for a longer time then it may yield invaluable insights into how the department has been operating.

Again, if we can continue with an example relating to transport costs. As vehicles get older, maintenance costs usually increase. If vehicles are purchased and kept for say five years, then maintenance costs will generally increase considerably in years four or five. Leasing a vehicle over three years may give increased costs in the short term, but yield longer term savings. An analysis of transport costs would therefore be a considerable advantage in the decision making process. Moreover, however well maintained the vehicle may be, as it becomes older, its fuel consumption will be greater than more modern vehicles and so an inter-relationship between age of vehicle, maintenance costs and fuel costs will be revealed.

REVENUES (OR INCOME)

Having examined past costs, now is the time to begin to explore revenue or income. In a department such as a DSO or an Architects Department which has already been charging for its services, data on revenues would be readily available. Even in those departments where charging for services has not been previously undertaken, it may be possible to ascribe some proxy charges for the major pieces of work undertaken. For example, in a Personnel Department which knows its overall costs for training activities carried out and the proportion of staff time allocated to this activity, it becomes possible to work out the proxy revenue which would have been earned had it been charged for at cost.

Comparison with what bought-in consultants had charged for a similar activity or which would be undertaken at "scale-fees" would yield valuable information.

To take another example, there is no reason why a committee clerk could not keep a full record of time spent on separate committees and other work. A charge could then be made to each user of that "service" on a proportional basis in order to cover the full costs incurred.

To summarise

Examine historical information on

    1   **Volumes of Work/Activity**

    2   **Costs of Levels of Activity**

    3   **Revenues or Income**

An examination of the above will alert an organisation to

1. How it has been developing over time

2. The **major** items of cost, revenue and work which may require further specific investigation

3. The inter-relationships and anomalies thrown-up by such data

4. A clear understanding of what drives the organisation

5. The possibility of producing some PROJECTIONS of such figures into the future (say years 1, 2 and 3) so as to get some feel for the financial health of the department

In making such PROJECTIONS, however, two points must be borne in mind.

1. That as the projections get further forward, say year 2 or year 3, they become less reliable because of changes which will inevitably take place, and

2. That using a simple PROJECTION of past figures will have the benefit of including "inflation" albeit at past rates.

With such PROJECTIONS one has a picture of the financial and workload future of the authority/department given for the moment that NO CHANGE takes place in:

1. Volumes of work undertaken

2. The costs associated with such work

3. The revenues obtainable from work carried out

It provides a bench-mark to judge what <u>new</u> costs may be incurred, what <u>new</u>

It provides a bench-mark to judge what new costs may be incurred, what new revenues might be obtained and what new or increased work activities might be undertaken to meet the department's objectives.

So far, we have left the term "OBJECTIVE" fairly loose and here we could be in danger of falling into the same trap that many local authority Business Plans have already fallen, namely, to leave objectives so ill-defined and non-specific that even if they were attainable no-one could know whether or not they had actually been attained.

The hall mark of a useful OBJECTIVE is that it is measurable, quantifiable or specifiable in some way so that one can know if it has been achieved.

It may therefore now be more useful to refer to TARGETS, the standard definition of which in Bussiness Planning terms is

> **"A numerical quantitative expression of an aim, ie an objective expressed in figures"**
>
> *(J.Argenti)*

We have to accept, however, that in some aspects of a local authority's work it is not always possible to express an objective in figures. What we would argue though, is that it is possible to make an objective specifiable enough to know whether it has been attained. For example, great strides have been made in the Regulation and Inspection Units of Social Services Departments to specify exactly what "care" might mean for a specific client. In effect, it describes in detail the activities and actions which should be taken to provide a particular kind of care. It is somewhat more difficult to monitor whether such actions have been carried out but at least some level of precision in specification has been reached.

> **Our definition of a TARGET would therefore become**
> **"An objective expressed in numerical, quantifiable or action terms".**

We have now reached what we would regard as the heartland of the analysis required to provide a Business Plan.

Given that it is inevitable that change will happen either induced by the management of the department or the external environment in which the department operates, we need to undertake a probing and rigorous examination of the FACTORS which might affect the authority/department's ability to reach its targets whether these are targets related to cost, revenues and volumes of work or targets deduced from the overall objectives of the authority/department.

The format we shall use for exploring the factors which could affect TARGETS will examine first the ORGANISATION itself and subsequently the ENVIRONMENT in which the organisation operates. Furthermore, for each FACTOR identified we need to examine:-

1.   The probability of the FACTOR occurring

2.   Its level of impact (ie high or low)

3.   Whether the impact is <u>negative</u> (ie, it adversely affects the ability to reach a target) or is <u>positive </u>(ie, it assists in reaching the target)

We shall outline here some of the FACTORS which, in a local government setting might affect the ability to reach targets but the list is by no means exhaustive. It could not be, for each <u>department</u> will have unique factors pertaining to it, and similarly the environment in which it operates will have certain unique factors extant only in that environment.

We would suggest that the first stage in carrying out this analysis is to convene a vertically-sliced group of participants to BRAINSTORM from their past experience and creativity a list of FACTORS which might conceivably be relevant to that particular department and environment. This should in preference be carried out in advance of our own particular list, for to do otherwise might dampen the creativity of your own group.

Moreover, people often say to us "Why 're-invent the wheel'; let us have a look at someone else's list or Business Plan". Apart from the fact that a Business Plan is unique and private to each organisation, this suggestion nullifies a significant purpose in going through the <u>process</u> of producing one; namely it is because people have examined their own organisation and environment and as a result have begun to believe that they indeed have "invented the wheel" that their Business Plan will have a vibrancy and commitment to it which otherwise would be unobtainable.

"Inventing the wheel" syndrome is an important phenomena in the preparation of a meaningful Business Plan for it creates a sense of ownership for all those involved.

WORK TO BE DONE
(Analysis of Factors)

1   **Generate a list of FACTORS unique to your own organisation and environment**

2   **Scan the list provided for additional FACTORS**

3   **For all FACTORS, identify -**

      i   **Probability of occurrence**
      ii   **Level of impact (high or low)**
      iii   **Direction of impact (negative or positive)**

The sophistication of the scoring method to be used is left to the reader. The essence is to identify the main issues arising.

NB This list will be used again later to identify

1. The STRENGTHS and WEAKNESSES of the ORGANISATION

2. The OPPORTUNITIES and THREATS existing in the ENVIRONMENT

3. The ACTIONS which the department will take to utilise strengths, overcome weaknesses, exploit opportunities and forestall or meet threats

SOME POSSIBLE FACTORS AFFECTING ABILITY TO REACH TARGETS			
THE ORGANISATION	Probability	Impact	Direction
1 THE PEOPLE			
1 Recruitment issues			
2 Retention issues			
3 Skill base issues			
4 Specialist skills (existing or new)			
5 Ability to cope with workload/volume of activity			
6 Absences (hours of attendance/holidays/use of overtime)			
7 Availability of training			
8 Consultation/negotiation issues			
9 Industrial relations/action			
10 Management structure			
11 Management style			
12 Opportunities for development and progression			
13 Willingness to be entrepreneurial			
2 PLANT EQUIPMENT AND MATERIALS			
1 Availability of specialist plant, equipment or materials			
2 Possibility of breakdown			
3 Possibility of damage			
4 Other unavailability			
5 Usage/wastage rates			
6 Warehousing facilities			
7 Balance of supplies v usage			
8 Transport planning and usage			
3 ADMINISTRATIVE REQUIREMENTS			
1 Timetable for tendering etc			
2 Skill base of support staff			
3 Payment/reward systems			
4 Availability of hardware/software systems			
5 Methods for dealing with central overheads			
6 Standing orders/financial regulations			

SOME POSSIBLE FACTORS AFFECTING ABILITY TO REACH TARGETS	Probability	Impact	Direction

THE ORGANISATION (cont.)

4   TRENDS IN FINANCE
1   Budgets availability for work activity
2   Pricing mechanism used (eg schedule of rates v daywork contracts)
3   Opportunity to spread oncosts/overheads
4   Economies of central purchasing
5   Availability of accurate data on costs, profits and losses
6   Trends in costs, revenues, profits and losses
7   Payment for work done
8   Payment systems

5   SERVICE DELIVERY ISSUES
1   Speed of response
2   Perceived effectiveness/complaints/customer satisfaction
3   Efficiency of provision
4   Efficiency in dealing with emergency situations
5   Attitude of staff to customers
6   Productivity
7   Operational methods
8   Work planning systems
9   Volumes of work
10   Flexibility of operation
11   Economies of scope
12   Inter-organisational synergy
13   Competitive advantage
14   Attainment of QA

6   FACILITIES
1   Office
2   Depot
3   Other establishments
4   Access
5   Layout
6   Location

7   POLITICAL ISSUES
1   New senior staff (eg Chief Executive or Chief Officer)
2   Changes in local political control
3   Changes in level of political activity
4   Changes in political priorities
5   Attitude toward specific   department(s)

SOME POSSIBLE FACTORS AFFECTING ABILITY TO REACH TARGETS			
THE ENVIRONMENT	Probability	Impact	Direction
1 GOVERNMENT			
1 Legislation - existing or potential			
2 Taxation/subsidy changes			
3 Availability of external funding			
4 Attitude toward specific service			
2 UK			
1 Economic changes			
2 Social changes			
3 Political changes			
4 Demographic changes			
3 TECHNOLOGY			
1 New products/services			
2 New materials			
3 New plant			
4 New equipment			
5 New processes			
6 Substitutes			
4 COMPETITORS			
1 Share of market issues			
2 Product/service obsolescence			
3 Major existing competitors			
4 Minor existing competitors			
5 New competitors			
6 Increase/decrease in competition			
7 Possible new markets			
8 Strengths and weaknesses of competitors			
5 LOCATION WITHIN ENVIRONMENT			
1 Concentration within area of possible customers			
2 Topography of market area			
3 Climate			
6 SUPPLIERS			
1 Price trends of materials/supplies			
2 Availability of materials/supplies			
3 Increasing/decreasing numbers of suppliers			
7 CUSTOMERS			
1 Total available market - growing/declining			
2 Top 10% of market			
3 Profile of customers/market groups			
4 Loyalty of customers to existing provider			
5 Yield/surplus on work undertaken			
6 What determines market share			
7 Requirement for success with customers			
8 Perceived effectiveness of service			
9 Perceived efficiency of service			

NB this list is not exhaustive - each user will identify additional FACTORS within their own organisation and their own environment.

Having completed the generation of FACTORS affecting the department, especially noting those with a high probability and a significant impact, one has gone part of the way to identify the strengths and weaknesses of the organisation and the opportunities and threats in the environment.

More work will have to be done later on

> (i) identifying the CAUSES of these phenomena
>
> (ii) the range of possible remedial actions and
>
> (iii) the chosen course of ACTION in respect of each one.

4. RESTRAINTS

Now is the time in the process to begin to determine what RESTRAINTS the department is expected to work under.

The definition of RESTRAINTS arrived at earlier was

> **"Those actions which   an organisation will take on moral or political grounds _whether or not_ they improve the ability to reach TARGETS"**

Again, like other aspects of the Business Plan, RESTRAINTS are unique to each organisation for they are imposed by the organisation itself. They are chosen ways of operating which the elected members and senior officers believe reflect the wishes of the electorate or their customers as expressed by the ballot box. Sometimes they will actually appear in the STATEMENT OF VALUES of the authority and its departments. Some of them may be seen as so important that they form part of the objectives of the authority or the department.

Nevertheless, they should always be seen for what they are and listed as such. To do otherwise, is to invite confusion for customers and for the workforce. The central purpose of a Business Plan is to gain clarity and thereby to challenge the assumptions, facts and the existing logic of the enterprise.

Some RESTRAINTS will already have been written down in that they appear in policy notes, committee minutes, manifestos, perhaps even in standing orders and financial regulations. Many other RESTRAINTS may never have been so clearly articulated but exist in unspoken assumptions, untested professional beliefs and the folklore of the organisation. At this stage they need identifying, bringing out into the open and thence challenging to change them, or to accept them for what they are and to cope with them.

The process again is to find some mechanism for generating a list of RESTRAINTS and then to explore each one for acceptance or rejection. At the end of this process it will be worthwhile to produce an interim document (which we refer to as a Position Statement on RESTRAINTS) listing all the existing RESTRAINTS. It may well appear as an appendix to the Business Plan. Like all the other parts of the Business Plan it will require regular review, for political and professional views will change, legislative and procedural requirements may change and organisational and environmental issues will change.

As practical examples of some of the RESTRAINTS which may be identified we offer the following list, but this is only a starting point for discussion

- Will the organisation knowingly break the law?

- Will it convert the entirity of its vehicle fleet to the use of lead free petrol?

- Will it tender for all contracts irrespective of whether they will make the rate of return?

- Will it take more health and safety precautions than the minimum standard required by the law?

- Will it mislead other departments, customers, the workforce etc or be secretive about its true intentions?

- Will it maintain national conditions of service?

- Will it unilaterally break existing negotiated agreements or custom and practice?

- Will it tender for work in the private sector?

- Will it aggressively tender for work from other neighbouring local authorities?

- Will it deliberately fail to submit tenders for some "in house" work?

- Will it take a high key market-strategy?

- Will the public and press be allowed to attend the board meeting?

- Will it provide information about its activities to local government agencies, eg CIPFA?

Clearly, some of the issues listed here as possible RESTRAINTS may be seen by some authorities as OBJECTIVES they wish to pursue. So be it. In a political organisation it would be surprising if it were otherwise but this does not deny the utility of surfacing them for analysis and consideration. Having produced a POSITION STATEMENT ON RESTRAINTS one has drawn the parameters within which the organisation will operate.

As an aid to collection of information to assist us in the whole of the preceding analyses, not merely the RESTRAINTS, we feel that the following questionnaire distributed to elected members responsible for the area of activity under consideration, and to every member of the workforce in the specific business units will provide rich information for consideration.

CHECKLIST FOR BUSINESS CENTRE STAFF

A   **Identify and write down the issues/problems relating to your own business centre for the following**

1 What are we good at?

     a   How good is productivity?

     b   How efficient are we?

     c   How profitable are we?

     d   How competitive are we?

     e   What are our weaknesses?

2 What do our customers think?

     a   Who are our customers?

     b   Do we know what they think about our effectiveness?

     c   Do we know what they think about our efficiency?

     d   How can we get improved feedback?

3 What are the threats and restraints?

     a   How does the law affect us?

     b   Do any Council policies hinder us substantially?

     c   Do Support Services provide the required support?

     d   Have we got all the resources we require?

     e   Do we need to consider any training requirements?

4 What opportunities should we grasp?

     a   How can we increase a market share?

     b   Can we provide any specialist services?

     c   Have we explored all avenues of work?

     d   How do we increase our volume of work?

5 Where can we improve?

    a   Can productivity be improved?

    b   Can the incentive bonus scheme be simplified while maintaining good productivity?

    c   What about working methods?

    d   How well are holidays planned?

    e   What is our sickness record?

    f   Can we improve on the use of transport?

    g   Can we plan the use of materials better?

    h   Have we got the best organisation to do the work?

    NB   *Set out a family tree and an age profile of your workforce.*

6 Does everyone know what is going on?

    a   What are the formal arrangements for consultation?

    b   How does information get passed on (either up or down)?

    c   Does the workforce feel involved and committed?

7 Do we get the right information?

    a   Can we find out regularly (monthly) what the financial state of our business is?

    b   Do we know regularly (weekly) what the productivity of the workforce is?

    c   Do we fully understand the information we already get?

    d   Do we know what the Council's policies and objectives are in relation to the work of our business centre?

    e   What do you feel are the restraints imposed upon us?

8 Who are our competitors?

    a   Who are our main competitors?

    b   What do you know about their products/services?

c   How do we feel they compare with ourselves?

d   What do we think are their

(i) strengths

(ii) weaknesses

B   In answering any or all of the above questions think about and set down priorities and timescales

1   How to improve feedback from customers

2   Training requirements

3   Simplifying the incentive bonus scheme

4   Improving productivity

5   Improving working methods

6   How to improve sickness records

7   Planning holidays

8   Better use of transport

9   Controlling material usage and wastage

10 An organisation chart to meet your requirements

11 How communications can be improved

12 What information you require, in what form and how frequently

13 How you can reduce costs

14 How you can increase work

15 How might you reduce the restraints upon you

We have listed here only the questions which might be useful to ask. If it were to be used as a proforma for replies, the layout of the questions would be crucial so as to leave space for replies.

This marks a mid-point in our exploration and analysis of the organisation; its objectives, its costs, revenues and volumes of work; the organisational and environmental factors which may affect it; and the restraints it is prepared to work under. Now we can begin to move to explore what actions can be taken to strengthen weaknesses, capitalise on strengths, forestall or deal with threats and exploit opportunities. From here on we are exploring the ACTIONS we are going to take and it is these ACTIONS which will form the bulk of the Business Plan which will be presented to elected members and to other interested parties.

5. Determining the Means/Actions by which Targets are to be Achieved

This step in the process of producing a Business Plan requires us to turn back to the analysis of FACTORS AFFECTING THE ABILITY TO ACHIEVE TARGETS and to examine and consider more fully those issues which we felt might have a high probability of occurring, and with a significant impact, upon the organisation.

If that impact was identified as positive ie it was beneficial to the organisation, we would be seeking ways of ensuring that it happened.

If the impact was negative ie damaging to the organisation, then we wold be seeking ways in which to forestall such occurrence or to take appropriate remedial action.

We need however, a systematic approach for dealing with each of the identified FACTORS. The approach we suggest is to take each FACTOR in turn and to:

> 1   **Describe the issue/problem**
>
> 2   **State the reasons/causes for its occurrence**
>
> 3   **List the possible actions which might be taken**
>
> 4   **Select the most appropriate course of action**

Let us say for example, that in our analysis of the ORGANISATION we had identified a high probability of there being difficulty in the recruitment of skilled staff and this would have a significant adverse effect upon the organisation, ie it was an organisational WEAKNESS.

Applying the above analysis to the issue we might arrive at the following statements:

1   Describe the Issue/Problem

There has been a long-standing difficulty in recruiting staff to the authority/ department. The problem extends to all grades of staff within the department but in particular to computer literate junior finance staff. The recently available population surveys shows that in our part of the UK the problem may worsen, with school leavers reducing by 10% over the next five years. This would lead to:

- unfilled vacancies, spreading workload over remaining staff

- increased claims for over-time working by remaining staff

- a worsening industrial relations climate

- failure to meet deadlines for essential financial work

- problems in fulfilling contract or service level agreement requirements

- lack of new entrants leading to long-term skills shortage

2 REASONS/CAUSES

1   Computer literate junior financial staff are drawn from a very local population area (approximately 10 miles radius), there being other centres of employment within a 20 mile radius

2   There are a number of other large private and public sector employers within our catchment

3   Our pay scales are comparable with other employers but the fringe benefits are not

4   Our skilled and experienced staff move to departments where at the moment they have greater career opportunities

5   We tend to advertise in the school-leavers job market too late in the year, therefore potential employees have been offered positions in other organisations before considering our own

3 POSSIBLE ACTIONS

1   Market the job opportunities in our department more frequently and much earlier in the job market year

2   Seek to increase the pay scales in shortage areas

3   Seek fringe benefits, eg

    - key workers housing

    - extension of car leasing to junior staff

    - free membership of BUPA etc

4   Increase our training programmes but with a contractual requirement for staff to stay 3 years with the department after completion of training

5   Increase the opportunities for such staff to develop and progress within our own department by increasing the amount of in-service training and to create promotion positions

4 Selected Action(s)

In essence, possibly a combination of options one and five re-stated as

> **We will market the job opportunities in our department more forcefully, in a slightly wider catchment and earlier in the job-market year**
>
> **We shall stress the in-service training opportunities and at an early date attempt to create better career progression for such staff within our own department**
>
> **We will monitor the effect over the next 12 months**

Option number two has been rejected as it will probably antagonise other departments and in any case may have "knock-on" effects.

Option number three is rejected because of "knock-on" effects and the Council's political objection to private health insurance.

Option number four is rejected on the advice of the Personnel Officer as it contravenes National Conditions of Service. (Query - do we have at some future date to consider moving away from National Conditions of Service?)

So here we have a set of ACTIONS which the department is going to take over the next 12 months and it will become one of a multitude of ACTIONS within its Business Plan.

Obviously, each of the WEAKNESSES in the Organisation needs to be taken in turn and explored in the same way with a course of ACTION chosen.

Applying the same process to one of the FACTORS we have earlier identified as a potential Organisational STRENGTH (ie it will assist us in reaching TARGETS) we might get an example like the following:

1 Describe the Issue/Problem

The productivity of the workforce is very high.

2 Reasons/Causes

During the 1980s the Council invested heavily in an exercise to improve productivity. Many hours of discussion and negotiations took place. There were many crisis points and for a period the industrial relations climate suffered. This traumatic experience was justified when the old mode of operating was broken and new working arrangements and practices put in place. Productivity dramatically improved and the industrial relations climate has now settled down with all parties recognising the benefits which have been obtained.   This productivity must be maintained and strengthened.

3 POSSIBLE ACTIONS

1   Maintain existing working arrangements

2   Maintain existing incentive payment systems

3   Challenge adverse comments on the utility of existing arrangements

4   Rethink incentive rewards if moves are made to change the system whereby work is ordered and charged for

5   Make certain that if new systems of ordering and charging are forced upon the department, proper consideration is given to the likely effects upon productivity

6   Institute productivity circles amongst the workforce to further improve upon our current position

4 SELECTED ACTION(S)

Options numbered one, two and three are discounted as no organisation can afford to stand still.

Option number five is not a sufficiently positive course of action to take.

A combination of option number four and option number six may well be the best course of action to take, ie rethink incentive rewards if moves are made to change the system whereby work/service is ordered and charged for. Institute productivity circles amongst the workforce to underline the importance of this FACTOR in the strength of our department. Productivity circles to be in place within three months.

This course of action now becomes one amongst many in our Business Plan.

Turning now to the THREATS in the environment and applying the same process:

1 DESCRIBE THE ISSUE/PROBLEMS

Currently there is a falling demand for one component of our service, which has in the past been an important part. This has adverse implications for the plant, equipment, facilities and staff utilitised in the provision of this part of our service. Moreover, demand is expected to fall by 5% per annum over the next five years.

It is a significant THREAT within our environment.

2 REASONS/CAUSES

(a)   Due to a tightening on local authority expenditure generally, the Council's budgets have been shrinking in real terms. The result is that less money is available for one of our components of service. The matter has been further exacerbated by a deepening recession, with little prospect of an early return to the original level.

(b)   The total market for a component of our service is falling (our percentage share of the market is steady) due to the rise in substitution services, ie other ways of providing the service.

3 POSSIBLE ACTIONS

1   Increase our percentage share of the falling market so as to maintain our facilities and staff

2   Improve the acceptability and effectiveness of this part of our service so as to compete more ably with the developing substitutes

3   Adapt our service by re-equiping and re-training our staff to provide this substitution service

4   Enter a joint venture with a major provider of subsitution services so that we may obtain expertise and knowledge and have some control over the speed at which substitute services affect our own service

4 SELECTED ACTION(S)

Option number four has been denied to the department by Council imposed RESTRAINTS on this sort of venture

> **As our existing component of service cannot in the long-term compete with, or be modified easily, because of its very nature, then in the short-term we will try to increase our share of the market so as to buy time for complete re-equipping and re-skilling of our workforce to other areas of activity.**

Similarly, for each perceived THREAT in the environment, the above analysis needs to be undertaken and where the THREATS can be forestalled or remedied then the selected ACTION will become part of the Business Plan.

Turning now to an example of OPPORTUNITIES in the environment:

1 DESCRIBE THE ISSUE/PROBLEM

The total budgets available for spending on a particular part of our service by other departments and other agencies has been expanding by about 10% pa in real terms over the past five years, and this trend looks as if it will continue for the next three years.

This is an OPPORTUNITY for us to increase the volume of work undertaken and hence revenues received.

2 REASONS/CAUSES

No clear data is available to explain this expansion of budgets but it is probably due to changing social and political values regarding the usefulness of this type of service. There seems to be an emerging philosophical belief that it is a "good thing" to be doing.

We must treat this development with some caution but nevertheless feel we should capitalise on this OPPORTUNITY at least in the short-term.

3 POSSIBLE ACTIONS

1.   Further research to more clearly identify the cause of this growth

2.   Accept the growth at face value and try to predict for how long it will continue

3.   Move more of our existing resources, both facilities and staff into this area of activity

4.   Begin to explore what implications for re-equiping and recruitment of staff this continued expansion may have

5.   Ignore the expansion on the basis that our resources are already stretched

4 SELECTED ACTIONS

Option number one seems a prudent course of action for it may give us some feel as to how long the trend may last. However, it should be linked to option number four, ie exploring the implications for re-equipping and recruitment of staff.

> Certainly, we do not wish to ignore this expansion even if resources are currently stretched, yet option number three is unwise at this early stage. Nevertheless, it is an OPPORTUNITY which must be further explored with a view to obtaining within the next twelve months a proportion of these increased budgets. If we gain more work of this nature we may have a broader basis over which to spread our on-costs and overheads.

	WORK TO BE DONE
	(Determining Actions)

1. Scan the list of FACTORS which you have already identified

2. Choose those which seem to you to be the most significant in terms of probability and impact

3. Describe the issue/problem

4. State the reasons/causes for its occurrence

5. List the possible actions which might be taken

6. Select the most appropriate course of action

This process of analysis will be applied to each FACTOR AFFECTING OUR ABILITY TO REACH TARGETS.

In the next chapter we will begin to examine the other aspects of service development.

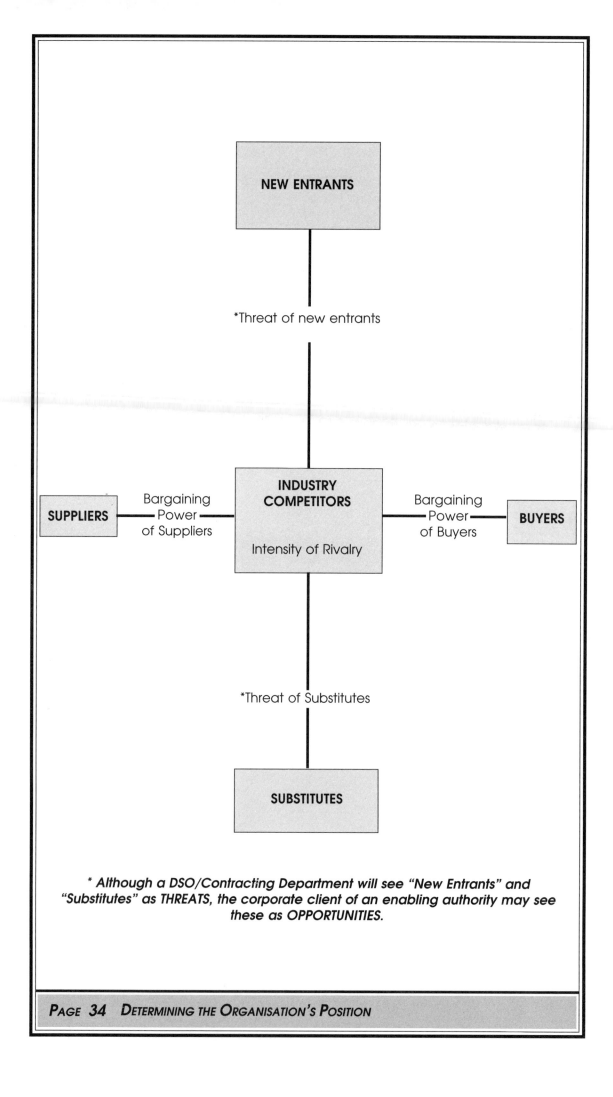

NEW ENTRANTS

*Threat of new entrants

SUPPLIERS

Bargaining
Power
of Suppliers

INDUSTRY
COMPETITORS

Intensity of Rivalry

Bargaining
Power
of Buyers

BUYERS

*Threat of Substitutes

SUBSTITUTES

* Although a DSO/Contracting Department will see "New Entrants" and "Substitutes" as THREATS, the corporate client of an enabling authority may see these as OPPORTUNITIES.

6. DETERMINING THE ORGANISATION'S POSITION WITHIN ITS ENVIRONMENT

So far we have applied this analysis only to our existing service activities and in relation to a fairly rudimentary exploration of the environment/market place in which our services might be provided. Now is the time therefore, to undertake a more sophisticated analysis of the DETERMINANTS of the organisation's POSITION within the environment. The principal determinants are represented in the diagram opposite.

There are a number of issues to be considered. The first relates to the RIVALRY amongst existing competitors. The INTENSITY of the RIVALRY is determined by a number of factors.

A   INTENSITY OF RIVALRY AMONGST EXISTING COMPETITORS DEPENDS UPON:

1   THE NUMBER OF EXISTING COMPETITORS

Where there is a large number of existing competitors, eg

- in the provision of residential accommodation for elderly people, or

- the provision of housing repairs to municipal housing,

then the position of the local authority may be relatively weak. This would be even more noticeable and influential if the competitors were of equal size and power but manifestly, in most instances, this is not so. In the first example, the local authority has the power to inspect and regulate such other providers and thereby exert a controlling influence over them. In the second example the local authority can so order its relationship with its own DSO, if it so wishes, to maximise its power in the marketplace.

2   THE SPEED OF GROWTH

Where growth in the market is slow, fights for market share are commonplace. In the sphere of "consultancy services" to local authorities, one might argue that growth, if not slow at the moment, will decline with increasing financial restraints over the foreseeable future. This will encourage increased competition and battles for market share amongst existing and new providers.

3 THE DEGREE OF DIFFERENTIATION

Where there is little or no differentiation between services, the service which customers require may be obtained from a number of sources eg architects and trade refuse collection. In this situation, the intensity of rivalry will be high.

4 THE ABSENCE OF SWITCHING COSTS

Where consumers of the service experience little or no penalty in moving from one supplier of service to another, then this increases the intensity of competition eg the recent changes in the education service allow parents to move a child from one school to another or even into a school in another education authority area.

In effect, there is virtually an absence of switching cost in this decision.

5 THE LEVEL OF FIXED COSTS EXPERIENCED BY PROVIDERS

Where fixed costs are high this creates a considerable temptation to reduce overall prices so as to achieve at least a marginal rate of return on these fixed costs eg uPVC factory and highways work, thereby heightening the rivalry between existing competitors.

6 THE SIZE OF INCREMENT IN CAPACITY

Where capacity to provide a service is increased only by large increments this increases the level of intensity of competition; eg if an additional, rather than a mere extension of a facility, is installed, (say for example a new uPVC manufacturing unit,) then this would augment existing capacity in a very significant way. It can disrupt the existing supply/demand balance and lead to periods of over capacity and a consequent tendency towards price-cutting. This can be exacerbated by the rigidity involved in narrow business centres.

7 THE MAGNITUDE/HEIGHT OF EXIT BARRIERS

Where exit barriers are high, perhaps due to loyalty to the service by policy makers or senior managers or due to the possession by the service of very specialised assets, then this also increases the intensity of competition eg the loyalty of elected members and officers to their own DSOs together with the specialist equipment they possess creates an enormous "exit barrier". In many instances this is so high that they are prepared to compete with the DSOs of neighbouring authorities to acquire that work. This can be true even where the rate of return on such work might only be at base levels, if such work would use up surplus capacity.

8   THE <u>DIVERSITY</u> OF THE RIVALS

Where the rivals are so diverse in political beliefs, values, strategies and even personalities, each perhaps having different views about competition, they continuously come into conflict with one another and with other agencies and become unable to differentiate between PRIMARY OBJECTIVES, SECONDARY OBJECTIVES and RESTRAINTS. In this situation confusion reigns but, nonetheless, it adds to the <u>intensity</u> of competition.

Whilst an organisation has to live with many of these factors, nevertheless, it may have some opportunity for improving the situation. It may try, for example, to increase the <u>differentiation</u> of the service they provide from that of other providers. For example,

- housing departments are trying to show to their tenants that the quality and type of services they provide is different from that of other organisations

- a department may be trying to increase the loyalty to the service it provides and attempt to raise the intangible switching costs of moving from one supplier to another eg on legal services or cost and works accounting

- a local authority may take a conscious decision not to compete with another local authority for a contract recognising the other local authority's high exit barriers and thereby avoid involvement in bitter price-cutting.

So far we have discussed only the INTENSITY of RIVALRY but there are four other determinants of the organisation's position within its environment/market place.

B   THE **THREAT** OF **NEW ENTRANTS** TO THE ENVIRONMENT/MARKET PLACE

"New entrants to a market place bring new capacity, the desire to gain market share and often substantial resources"

(Michael J Porter)

It is the BARRIERS to entry and the REACTION from existing providers that determines entry. The sources of BARRIERS to entry are the following:

1   THE CAPITAL REQUIREMENTS

Where the capital requirements create high cost, then a barrier to entry exits, eg refuse collection if competitors are forced to buy depot facilities and specialist equipment as opposed to leasing it.

2   THE <u>ECONOMIES</u> OF SCALE INVOLVED FOR THE EXISTING PROVIDER

Where the economies of scale are currently available to an existing provider and those pertain to distribution channels, as well as the other components of a service, then this is a barrier to entry for potential new entrants. For example, the level, quality and numbers of staffing necessary to provide a comprehensive "casework" service in a local authority social services department may deter entry by some agencies.

3   THE SERVICE IS <u>DIFFERENTIATED</u>

Where the service is differentiated and there is high customer loyalty, then this creates another barrier to entry.

For example, the policy advice offered to committees by a competent legal service would be rarely available amongst possible new entrants to the market-place. Furthermore, a history of sound advice would act as a deterrent to a local authority's "spending department" which was considering the possibility of seeking to 'buy' such a service from outside the local authority. Conversely, a history of poor advice and inadequate advocacy may persuade a department at an early date to seek such service from outside the local authority - RESTRAINTS permitting.

4   THE <u>COST</u> ADVANTAGES:

(a)   arising from specialist knowledge

Where the existing provider has specialist knowledge, it will act as a deterrent to possible new entrants. For example,

- the specialist education knowledge existing in the advisory functions of an education department

- the "experience curve" existing in a grounds maintenance section ie experience of the problems and difficulties pertaining to particular ground terrains.

(b)   residing in purchase of ASSETS at pre-inflation prices

For example, local authorities have, by the mechanism of the compulsory purchase order, acquired over many years valuable land upon which to develop. Where these have involved "unfit housing" then local authorities have acquired vast tracts of city centre land at nominal uncleared site-values upon which to build new establishments. Services currently operating from such establishments have thus acquired their assets well below market prices which could not be matched by new entrants.

Another category of cost advantage exists where a local authority has already acquired quality assurance certification for a particular part of its service.

Rivals must obtain this level before beginning to compete effectively and again this acts as a deterrent to entry.

5 THE EXISTENCE OF DEVELOPED DISTRIBUTION CHANNELS

Where distribution channels for a service already exist, the new competitor may be forced to break into this distribution channel or to create its own. In a way, the existing set of networks and contacts between central service departments and "spending" departments is a distribution channel for service, and a new competitor has to incur the cost of gaining these contacts and developing a network. Clearly, this may again deter entry.

6 THE EXISTENCE OF REGULATORY CONTROL

Where licensing and regulatory powers are vested in a local authority, this can create a significant barrier to entry eg: taxi and private hire licensing. Similarly, the requirement for practising certification eg, solicitors, social workers, environmental health-officers, creates a further significant barrier to entry for possible competitors.

7 THE REACTIONS OF EXISTING PROVIDERS

The anticipated REACTIONS of existing providers will also influence the decisions of possible new entrants. They are likely to be at least cautious of entry if:

(a)   The present provider possesses political will, power, influence and resources to protect their position and clearly, in many fields of activity, the local authority as the present monopoly provider of certain services is exactly in this position.

For example, what new entrant would willingly take on the might of a local authority deeply committed to maintaining in-house provision in an attempt to usurp the present provider. This is not to say that a new entrant will not be tempted, but it certainly provides a barrier.

(b)   The present provider is likely, under pressure, to enhance their competitive advantage by cost-cutting exercises so as to maintain their market share. The reality of local government is most probably that the threat of possible competition has so sharpened its costing structure and its competitive edge that only in a minority of situations will it experience severe competition. The barriers to entry are very high if the local authority is prepared to recognise them and act in a concerted way.

(c)   The available growth in a market, if poor, deters a new entrant who recognises that their arrival will add to capacity and in turn adversely affect the performance of all parties.

This requires that potential new entrants possess a sophisticated analysis of the market place, which many do not. There are widespread examples of new entrants _feeling_ rather than _analysing_ that there is market share available. They enter the market taking only a small part of it and soon leave again. But it is still to the disadvantage of existing providers who have had to reduce price below economic levels or take other action to see-off the new competitor.

Clearly conditions can change and in one's analysis of the market some element of looking into the future, ie prediction, is necessary. For example, the possibility of new legislation emerging following a response to some inquiry may well alter certain barriers to entry. If one predicted that in two years time all central service departments would be statutorily required to produce a 20% surplus on costs, then this would significantly affect new entrants and the barriers deterring them.

Strategic decisions affecting a large segment of existing providers can have a major impact upon the threat of entry. For example, if a conurbation wide group of local authorities jointly took a strategic decision not merely to refrain from competing with one another for work, but also to go further and pool resources in certain areas of activity, then this would have the effect of strengthening the barriers to entry.

In Business Planning terms, this is one of the most powerful arguments for local authorities to act together over a whole range of activities so as to decrease the level of competition from possible new entrants. It is a mechanism available and widely used by the private sector and currently, given goodwill and political compatibility between local authorities, is a perfectly possible strategy for local government to adopt.

C THE SUPPLIERS OF GOODS OR SERVICES TO AN ORGANISATION ALSO AFFECT THE ORGANISATION'S ABILITY TO COMPETE AND ITS ABILITY TO ACHIEVE ITS OBJECTIVES. THE POWER OF THE SUPPLIERS IS DEPENDENT UPON:

1   THE DOMINATION OF SUPPLIES

A very few companies can dominate supplies, particularly if they possess a concentration greater than the organisations to which they sell.

This is true of the computer hardware industry insofar as it sells to 500 local authorities. It is also the raison d'être for the establishment of region wide purchasing organisations by local authorities to offset supplier power (eg ESPO - Eastern Shires Purchasing Organisation). One imagines that this mechanism will be increasingly utilised by local authorities so as to place themselves in a more competitive situation and to make them less dependent upon the power of suppliers to determine their success.

2   A <u>UNIQUE</u> OR <u>DIFFERENTIATED</u> PRODUCT OR SERVICE

For example, there is a limited number of companies producing some of the very complex equipment used by the fire service. Moreover, there is an investment by the user in the training of the mechanics/ fitters to maintain and service such equipment. To an extent, therefore, the user becomes tied to a particular company and to change suppliers involves at least a "switching cost" or even the unavailability of particular equipment from any other source.

3   THE <u>ABSENCE</u> OR PAUCITY OF SUBSTITUTES

Long wheel base extended limousines purchased for civic use is an example of the local authority market (indeed the entire market) being dependent upon only two suppliers. Not only are there merely two suppliers but it is difficult to imagine a <u>substitute</u> conveyance possessing quite the same attributes.

4   THE SUPPLIERS ABILITY TO <u>INTEGRATE FORWARDS</u> INTO THE LOCAL AUTHORITY'S BUSINESS

This acts as a check on the authority's ability to improve the terms upon which it purchases services or goods from its supplier. This factor would be a significant potential threat to social services departments were it not that the regulations and inspection arm of a social service department is in effect a "judge and jury" in its own cause. Were it to be made a wholly independent "third-party" organisation, then current private sector providers of "care" places would have significant power as to the prices they charged the local authority for places provided. They would also possess the threat of forward integration into the local authority's business. For the time being, this is not an option they could credibly pursue as the real power resides with the regulatory arm of the social services department.

5   THE <u>PURCHASER ORGANISATION</u> IS A RELATIVELY <u>SMALL</u> CUSTOMER

It is therefore of only limited consequence to the supplier eg; the supply of general stationery to an electoral registration section. In this situation, the supplier is in a more powerful position than the buyer.

D   THE POWER OF CUSTOMER/BUYER GROUPS IS DEPENDENT ON:

1   THE <u>VOLUME</u> OR <u>CONCENTRATION</u> OF PURCHASES MADE

Where the CUSTOMER/BUYER buys or receives a large volume of the local authority's output of service eg a local authority housing department which buys/receives 75% of the housing repair service of the DSO then the housing department is in a powerful position and can to some extent dictate price and quality of the service it receives. The supplier, (the DSO) having high staff costs, (perhaps exacerbated by a RESTRAINT of no-redundancy) will wish to keep capacity filled. If the supplier (the DSO) had the ability to take-on or lay-off staff at will then the power of the buyer is diminished. Incidentally, this highlights the importance of analysing and perhaps challenging the RESTRAINTS an organisation is required to work under.

2   THE STANDARDISATION OF THE PRODUCT/SERVICE

If the product/service is undifferentiated, ie in no way unique, the customer/buyer can easily go elsewhere for alternative supplies. Insofar as local authority departments are buyers of the printing service of a DSO there is usually surplus capacity in this market and a wide range of alternative suppliers of printing services. If the DSO printing service has a sophisticated technology or expertise not widely available to other suppliers, this will enhance its service and customers become locked in and therefore the power of the customer is lessened.

3   THE PRICE SENSITIVITY OF THE PRODUCT/SERVICE.

If the customer pays dear or perceive that they pay dear for a product or service which is an <u>essential</u> part of their own activity then the customers will work hard to seek an alternative supplier at similar quality but lower cost or same cost and better quality. Presumably, this is one of the phenomena underlying the movement to the local management of schools. The customers pay dear for this service and will move their child to achieve better quality. Conversely, if the value or cost to the customers is only minimal then customers are usually less price sensitive and therefore exert less power. For example, where swimming costs in pools within reasonable distance of each other are similar, then "regular" customers are unlikely to change on price grounds alone.

4   THE <u>PROFITS/REVENUES</u> WHICH THE <u>CUSTOMERS</u> RECEIVE FOR THEIR OWN ACTIVITIES

If the profits/revenues are low this in turn creates considerable pressure for customers to lower their own purchasing costs. For example, this would be true of a DSO which was fighting hard to make its rate of return, for it would then constantly challenge the overhead charges made by central departments. If its rate of return was high, it would generally be a little less sensitive to such charges. Similarly, a personnel department making large surpluses from its training activities would not question too closely the hire payments made to the library service for the hire of video training materials. If surplus was low they would seek to minimise hire fees and all other input costs.

5   THE <u>QUALITY</u> OF THE PRODUCT/SERVICE RECEIVED IN RELATION TO THE CUSTOMERS' REQUIREMENTS

If the quality of the product/service received is high, then the customer may not be price sensitive but will be **quality** sensitive. For example, the carpenters/joiners in a local authority DSO concerned with housing maintenance will regard as crucial to their own success and performance, the **quality** of the materials (say window frames) which they receive from the joiners shop/uPVC unit. The ultimate customer's (the house tenant) impression of the fitter's work will be influenced by the quality of the fitment installed.

6   THE ABILITY TO POSE A CREDIBLE THREAT OF BACKWARD INTEGRATION ie to make/provide, as customers, the product/service themselves

The classic example of this phenomena in local authority terms is the desire of "spending" departments to have their own in-house accountants, personnel officers, lawyers etc ie the spending department as buyer/customer is integrating backwards to provide itself with its own accounting, personnel, legal advice service etc. This intention is subverted to an extent in the world of the local authority by such staff being required to be accountable "professionally" to the residual organisation at the centre.

Another example, is the threat to **opt-out** a school from LEA control. The essence of the argument is that if the LEA as a supplier/provider cannot produce the service at a cost or quality demanded by the customer, then the customer will arrange to have it provided on an opted-out basis. This is only an incidental point, but it reveals how the classical texts on business planning and marketing have influenced, over recent years, the developments in thinking about how local authority services shall be provided.

E   THE POWER OF SUBSTITUTES IS DEPENDENT UPON:

1   THE RELATIVE <u>PRICE-PERFORMANCE</u> OF THE SUBSTITUTE PRODUCE/SERVICE.

For example, if private sector training consultants have a uniform standard charge for the service they provide to "spending" departments this will limit the potential of an in-house training unit either to expand its service or to make an increased surplus on its existing activities.

Unless it can upgrade the quality of the service provided or more especially differentiate its service by its marketing activity, then it will suffer.

Obviously, the more clear-cut the price performance trade-off available from SUBSTITUTES the more the in-house unit will suffer in surplus and potential growth. Substitute services/products not only limit surplus and growth potential in normal times, but they also reduce the available excess surplus which might be produced when there is a large demand for an activity.

For example, there has been a very significant growth in recent times for "Assertiveness" training but the ability of an in-house unit to capitalise on this trend by raising fees and increasing revenue is dampened by the number of consultants identifying this trend and moving into this area of training activity.

2 THE SWITCHING COSTS INVOLVED FOR BUYERS/CUSTOMERS.

Often there is a penalty in costs (or in some other way) involved in moving to the use of a substitute. If this cost is absent then the power of substitutes is increased.

For example, if a "spending" department wished to change architects half-way through a project then manifestly it would seem some costs or difficulties would be involved. If the incoming architect, however, can show that such costs will be picked up in some way by the extra quality and speed of service they can provide, then the substitute has minimised the switching costs and thereby increased their power in relation to the customer.

A further example might be the local authority department which has a limited term contract with a supplier for a product or service and the contract has reached termination. In this case the cost of moving to a substitute may be almost nil.

3 THE BUYER/CUSTOMER WILLINGNESS/PROPENSITY TO SUBSTITUTE

If there is no loyalty or commitment to an existing service supplier then substitution service suppliers are in a powerful position.

For example, those other agencies which entered the field with a view to managing municipal housing stocks felt that there was little loyalty or commitment to the existing landlord, (the local authority).

The need to ballot tenants sensitised the tenants to the service provided by the local authority as a landlord and the residual loyalty felt towards the local authority meant that no change in management arrangements took place. In essence, there was no willingness to substitute.

Having identified the forces which effect competition and their underlying causes, one is in a much better position to determine the feasibility of moving into new areas of activity, such new areas of activity being analysed and chosen solely to assist the authority in meeting its declared objectives.

7. NEW AREAS OF ACTIVITY BEING ANALYSED AND CHOSEN SOLELY TO ASSIST THE AUTHORITY IN MEETING ITS DECLARED OBJECTIVES

Earlier, we identified the strengths and weakness of the organisation and the opportunities and threats in the environment in relation to existing areas of activity. Now is the appropriate time to extend this analysis to the six strategies which a local authority can adopt to deal with new ventures. The six strategies are:

1 **Market penetration**
(to increase its share of an existing market of provision)

2 **Market extension**
(to put existing activities into new markets)

3 **Product/service development**
(to refine an existing or develop a new service activity for its existing market)

4 **Diversification of activities**
(so as to provide new service activities to new groups of consumers)

5 **Integration backwards**
(to secure control over sources of supply of resources)

6 **Integration forwards**
(to secure control over the need for its activities)

For example's sake, we shall take in turn from our hypothetical local authority a WEAKNESS, a STRENGTH, an OPPORTUNITY and a THREAT and apply it to the six possible strategies to ascertain what MEANS might be available to achieve our OBJECTIVE

A. WEAKNESS - RECRUITMENT DIFFICULTY

1 MARKET PENETRATION (ie increase share of existing market)

As we are already experiencing difficulty in the recruitment of computer literate junior finance staff and this difficulty affects the whole of the market area, it would seem likely that it will also affect our competitors. Whilst we can lessen to a limited extent this weakness, it is also likely that similar ACTIONS will be taken by our competitors.

It would not seem likely therefore, that at this stage, market penetration was an easy possibility.

If we could substantially increase salaries, fringe benefits and career development opportunities we might achieve penetration for a short period, say twelve months. However, this would have a precedental effect upon other departments of the local authority. This does not seem a very feasible course of action for the time being. *(NO ACTION)*

2 MARKET EXTENSIONS (ie existing activities into new markets)

To try to put our existing activities into new markets when we are bedevilled by this recruitment issue is again, not a very feasible option. Indeed to do so, may increase our difficulties because competitors in the **wider new market** may not be incurring this disadvantage. Further information collection will be necessary on the environmental conditions pertaining in the new market area before we could consider this option further. *(ACTION 12 MONTHS)*

3 SERVICE DEVELOPMENT (ie refined or new service into existing market)

Further development of our service activities in such a way as to lessen our dependence upon computer based systems, at least for a period of time. Although this development would tend to fly in the face of general tendencies, this might give us the opportunity to put a new service on the ground which meets the requirements of our customers.

Further attention must be given to generating a list of new activities which **lessen** our dependence upon computer literate junior finance staff. *(ACTION 6 MONTHS)*

4 DIVERSIFICATION (ie new service activities to new groups of customers)

This is a more difficult strategy to undertake, for whilst we have ideas about how our present activities may be refined or new activities created, we have less knowledge about the needs of new customers. Until a customer analysis is carried out it would be imprudent to think of diversification at this time. It may be possible in the future. *(ACTION IN TWELVE MONTHS TIME)*

5 INTEGRATION BACKWARD (ie to secure control over supply of resources)

This action would seem to be a distinct possibility and has already been identified when considering existing activities. Indeed, as the principal resources of our department are the staff resources, they are crucial to any existing or new activities. This would suggest that we give more thought to -

- the provision of in-house training schemes;

- liaison with local and regional colleges of further and higher education;

- take a pro-active role in developing new courses at such institutions even to the extent of pump-priming some activities.

Furthermore, far greater involvement between the staff of such colleges and the staff and work of our department must commence at an early date. This will reduce the criticism from staff currently under training that much of what they receive is somewhat theoretical and does not touch upon the day-to-day work problems they experience. There may also be the opportunity of shared secondment of staff in both directions to increase knowledge about our respective organisations.

To thus secure greater control of the source of supply of at least some of our staff is more valuable and more feasible than backward integration for other components of our resourcing. *(ACTION AT AN EARLY DATE)*

---

6   INTEGRATION FORWARD (ie to secure control over demand for activity)

Only insofar as other departments of the local authority are our customers for certain activities we undertake, would it be possible to consider forward integration. What is more, this would require a re-organisation of departments with all the vested interests pertaining to that course of action.

It is not an option which could be pursued now or in the foreseeable future.

There is a chance perhaps, of making more captive our existing captive markets by seeking a complete ban on their opportunity to seek alternative or substitute suppliers. This, however, would contravene one of the political RESTRAINTS imposed upon all departments by the present Council to the effect that they should always be prepared to consider potential out-house suppliers. If there is a change in political control then this RESTRAINT may be challengeable. *(NO ACTION AT PRESENT)*

B. <u>STRENGTH</u> - HIGH PRODUCTIVITY OF WORKFORCE

1   MARKET PENETRATION

So long as we take the ACTIONS described earlier when considering our existing activities, so that we may maintain our high productivity, this will give us a useful spring board to increase our share of the market. Our productivity is higher than our competitors and this strength gives us a distinct competitive advantage. It may even be possible over time to "see-off" some of the weaker competitors thereby further increasing our market share. *(ACTION IMMEDIATELY)*

2   MARKET EXTENSION

Whilst superficially it is attractive to use our high productivity to put our existing activities into new markets, staff time and energy will have to be utilised to explore the new markets. Notwithstanding that it is senior staff with market research responsibilities who will undertake most of this work, some residual workload and therefore staff time will have to come from existing production staff. This could marginally affect their present level of productivity and must therefore be carefully monitored. With this proviso, however, market extension seems a distinct possibility. *(ACTION 6 MONTHS)*

3   SERVICE DEVELOPMENT

Our high productivity also gives us the opportunity to consider refined or new services to our market/customers. Demand is developing for a new range of advisory activity which we have not previously provided but which the workforce have the knowledge and skills to provide. Obviously, some attenuation of our existing productivity will occur, but again if carefully monitored should not significantly reduce our overall productivity. Moreover, as customers are **first** approaching us to provide this service it reveals some degree of loyalty to us. So long as we do not get over-stretched and our pricing policy for the new service is appropriate, this seems a feasible option. *(ACTION IMMEDIATELY)*

4   DIVERSIFICATION

The opportunities already outlined, if taken, will probably help us to achieve our overall objectives and to move to providing **new** services in **new** markets would be a somewhat risky venture. We would consider it only if other avenues to achieve our objectives were not possible.

5   INTEGRATION BACKWARD

Our high productivity is dependent upon no significant alteration to existing incentive schemes nor to the methods of ordering and charging for work. It would be possible to integrate backwards and obtain our own work study staff so as to challenge with expertise any proposals for change coming from the central personnel department. This would be costly. It may also generate tensions not currently existing between the department and the "centre" and therefore, would not seem a prudent course to follow. It is imperative however, that senior management staff of the department keep a watchful eye on any development that takes place in respect of these issues.

Discussions with elected members as to the absolute necessity of maintaining existing arrangements must be undertaken. *(ACTION IMMEDIATELY)*

6   INTEGRATION FORWARD

The only opportunity for this to occur would be if we could "advance earmark" either volumes of work or budgetary commitments so that we both know of and control work to be done at some future date. This would be highly desirable, for it may give us the opportunity to further increase our productivity by influencing

- when such work is carried out

- the pace at which it is undertaken

- the quantity of work to be done in a given time period.

This would enable us to schedule work at the optimum rate. It will be difficult to achieve unless the customer has total confidence in our ability to deliver the service in the way they want. It is not perhaps a realistic way forward at the moment but if customer confidence further increases it may be an option to pursue in the future. *(ACTION - KEEP UNDER REVIEW)*

C. THREAT - IN ENVIRONMENT

Falling demand for one component of our service (5% pa) caused by an increase in the availability of substitution services

1   MARKET PENETRATION

By definition, it is going to be difficult, even pointless, in the long run to achieve market penetration for a component of our services that is already declining at a rate of 5% per annum.

On the other hand, we thought earlier, that if we could arrest this trend for a short period, say 12 months, ie; to actually increase our market share by 5% of this falling market, this would buy us time for the re-equipping and re-skilling of our workforce. This will require us in the first instance to increase our volume of promotional activity and to make certain that existing customers continue to make use of our service.

We must re-assure them that the service will remain available to them as long as they feel they want it. We must then deliver on this promise so as not to contravene a self-imposed RESTRAINT to the effect "that we will not deliberately mislead our customers".

Furthermore, the existing quality of the service must not be impaired, so as to maintain customer loyalty for the time when our own produced substitute service is available. *(ACTION - THIS IS ONLY A SHORT-TERM MEASURE).*

2   MARKET EXTENSION

Some limited opportunity might exist for putting this component of our service into a wider market but again, this will probably be a short-term measure. Moreover, the level of promotional activity required may not justify this approach for the market areas which we would have to approach are probably already moving to substitute services. Indeed, we may prejudice our future reputation by being perceived to vigorously pursue what some people would regard as an obsolescent component of service. It is hardly in accord with our belief that we would seek to be a leading-edge service provider.

3   SERVICE DEVELOPMENT

Insofar as we can re-equip and re-skill our workforce to produce a new substitute service, we could be said to be involved in service development. This will take time and financial resources.

The minimum time required would be approximately nine months and the maximum time twelve months. There will be £100,000 of redundant equipment and facilities which must be covered in the budget for the forthcoming financial year. Current estimates suggest that £25,000 of training activity needs to be undertaken in the same period to re-skill the workforce. Had there been a possibility of compulsory redundancy (a RESTRAINT of no compulsory redundancy) this training figure could have been reduced to £15,000 as we could buy-in some of the skills we need.

Further work will have to be done to specify the exact equipment and training needed, but this is a feasible way forward to remedy the threat in the environment which otherwise would prevent us from reaching our objectives. *(ACTION IMMEDIATELY)*

4   DIVERSIFICATION

In some ways this threat of falling market is also an **opportunity** in that if we re-equip and re-skill to provide a substitute service, we can put it into new markets. This will require market and customer analysis and dependent upon what that research reveals, a considerable level of promotional activity. This really cannot commence until we are confident about the quality of our substitution service and have developed new distribution channels. It will require six months from now to analyse the possible markets.

5   INTEGRATION BACKWARD

In many ways this would have been the easiest option for we would have acquired knowledge, expertise and facilities overnight. This is denied by the existence of a council RESTRAINT on joint ventures with private sector firms. Should this situation arise again, then we must lobby to get this particular RESTRAINT removed, for it is damaging our ability to respond quickly to changes in the market/customer demand.

6   INTEGRATION FORWARD

Not a possibility in this situation.

D. OPPORTUNITY - IN ENVIRONMENT

Total available budget expanding at 10% pa in real terms for foreseeable future. Opportunity to increase volume of service activity provided.

1   MARKET PENETRATION

The existence of increasing budgets for a service activity we are currently providing is a case par excellence for market penetration to ensure that we obtain the totality of the increasing budget. The uncertainty lies in how long this trend will last, which may be illuminated by research into its causes. Clearly, existing customers must have their needs fulfilled but we must take vigorous action to ensure that service standards do not fall and enter early negotiation with budget-holders, playing up the strengths of our organisation to fulfil their needs.

Information about competitors may have a value, especially an understanding of their organisational weakness. More data on competitor weaknesses may possibly be culled from our workforce. (See questionnaire)

With caution we will move a small proportion of staff and facilities into this component of service to meet our anticipated increase in demand. As a matter of urgency, data must be collected so as to explain this phenomena and plans put in hand to further increase the volume of activity we can undertake. *(ACTION IMMEDIATELY)*

2   MARKET EXTENSION

In the long-term there may be some spin-off benefits in that the increased demand for this component of our service may be able to be put into a wider market, but not at this stage. *(CONSIDER THIS ISSUE AT NEXT REVIEW OF BUSINESS PLAN).*

3   SERVICE DEVELOPMENT

Whilst it may not be possible at the moment to provide a new service to the existing market, nevertheless, we must keep closely tuned to what existing customers are saying to us.

Customer surveys may give us leads as to how we may refine our existing service. This will increase our ability to obtain the totality of the increasing market.

4   DIVERSIFICATION

It would seem most imprudent to seek diversification at this time. It can always be reversed at some future date if we felt that too many resources were going into market penetration whilst we were still uncertain of the causes in the growth.

5   INTEGRATION BACKWARD

Not a necessary option in this area of activity at the moment unless some difficulty is experienced in obtaining resources to meet the increased demand (eg difficulty in obtaining additional skilled staff, or imperfections in the Service Level Agreements). This would direct attention to increasing in-house training activity, or revising the Service Level Agreements.

6   INTEGRATION FORWARD

As a complementary action to market penetration but undertaken in a rudimentary way, there is a crucial need to get closer to the customer, even if no opportunity exists for "taking-over" their demand for service.

Here we have given examples of how the analysis might be used, and the *notes* which might arise, from the examination of just one strength, one weakness, one opportunity and one threat in relation to the strategies available. In practice, each of the FACTORS affecting ability to achieve OBJECTIVES which have a significant probability of occurring, and a significant IMPACT, whether positive or negative, need testing out against the six strategies which an organisation can adopt to meet its objectives.

To summarise,

The position which we have now reached in our exploration is as follows:

1   Clarification and Agreement on Primary and Secondary Objectives

2   (a) Analysis of past COSTS, REVENUES AND VOLUMES OF WORK

(b) Projection forward of this data (assuming as a CONTROL - NO CHANGE)

3   (a) Identification of FACTORS affecting ability to reach OBJECTIVES

(b) Determination of Probability, Significance and Direction of Impact

(c) Construction of Cross Impact Analysis to identify inter-relationships

4   Determination of RESTRAINTS existing

5   Analysis of the FORCES affecting competitive position

6   Application of significant FACTORS to the six available strategies

This leaves us with a very long list of ACTIONS which might possibly be taken to achieve our OBJECTIVES. Indeed, the bulk of the analysis and exploration has now been completed.

In a way, the process we have adopted is analogous to the major overhaul of a motor vehicle before it commences a momentous journey. The power plant, (the engine of the organisation) is its resources. The gear box is the organisation's Business Plan - it transmits the power of the organisation toward the destination it wishes to reach.

Taking this analogy a little further, we have dismantled the gearbox into its various components. We have identified those which we might wish to re-profile, repolish, repair or discard. We have now to take a decision in respect of each component as to its future, for so far we have only noted what **possible** actions might be taken. It may, of course, be too expensive to take every action which we would like, and some components which initially we thought we would replace may simply have to be repaired.

A final decision will have to be made. Moreover, some actions might be more appropriate than others and, on occasion, two or more linked components will have to be replaced together. The combined effect will thereby be greater than the sum of the individual action which might be taken in respect of each component.

Each component is now laid out before us. We have detailed notes on each of them.

Which components fit together?
Are there any which have been mislaid?
Which form inter-locking sub-assemblies?
How shall we fit them together?

These are the questions with which we must now be concerned.

If we apply these ideas to our local authority, in many cases an individual action will solve an individual problem but sometimes actions taken in combination are more appropriate. This was identified earlier when examining specific issues. But to take another example from the earlier stage, the following possible individual actions were identified.

Increase our share of the market
Cut production and re-deploy existing staff
Strengthen our promotion section

These are three seemingly inconsistent actions but there may be a way of finding one action that resolves all three issues eg enter a joint venture with a neighbouring local authority so increasing the joint authorities share of the total market, using up the neighbouring authorities spare capacity and acquiring the expertise of their well-staffed marketing and promotional section.

In this way there is benefit to both organisations (NB. The RESTRAINT on joint ventures mentioned earlier was only in respect of joint ventures with **private** sector bodies).

For each action proposed, a final set of test questions might be appropriate - in effect putting oneself in the position of devil's advocate - to ensure that your final recommendations are as robust and rigorous as possible. *These questions are set out in list form on Page 56.*

One step remains before final assembly and that is to COST the IMPLICATIONS in RESOURCE TERMS of the ACTIONS proposed and to compare them with the PROJECTIONS made earlier for Years 1,2 and 3.

The same headings for COSTS, VOLUMES OF WORK and if appropriate, REVENUES can be used to make this comparison.

The gaps (positive or negative) between the earlier PROJECTIONS and the RESOURCE IMPLICATIONS of the proposed ACTIONS will give clear indications as to what resources can be switched from one ACTION to another, what further funding may be necessary, and which ACTIONS may have to be abandoned or modified in such a way as to meet part of an objective at lesser cost. We may not always have the resources to buy a new primary gear for our gearbox but have to settle for it being re-profiled. At the next major overhaul financial circumstances may be different and it can then be replaced by a new component.

The way is now clear for final decisions to be made - decisions which may require changes in organisational structure. Heaven forbid that we should advocate structural change in organisations which seem to be undergoing permanent structural change almost ad nauseam, with the consequential disruption of effort and skill which this entails. But the reality is that if, for example, a department is going, for the first time, to take on a major marketing initiative reporting directly to the Chief Officer, then a new sub-unit may be necessary to develop this activity - this inevitably will have some effect on the organisational structure of the department.

The final activity in the main part of the Business Plan process is to produce SPECIFICATIONS FOR ACTION.

For example, if it has been noted earlier that a particular establishment was inappropriately located, inadequate in size, layout, and facilities, the chosen action to be taken might involve building a new establishment of adequate size and layout, with a full range of necessary facilities, and located in another part of the local authority area. Clearly if a decision to proceed is taken, one then has to specify a number of items

1   Who will be in charge of the project?

2   What type and size the establishment will be, and the cost?

3   When is it to be completed?

4   Where is it to be built?

5   Why is it to be built? - presumably to facilitate a primary or secondary objective

6.   How will it be built?

The details as to the building materials to be chosen, the contractor to choose etc will form part of the business centre Business Plan for the person in charge of the project.

Similarly a SPECIFICATION FOR ACTION is required for each of the chosen actions that the authority has decided to take to reach its objectives. Each specification will state WHO, WHAT, WHEN, WHERE, WHY and HOW and in turn will become the targets of business centres of the department.

It is also imperative that if RESTRAINTS exist as they most assuredly will do, then SPECIFICATIONS FOR ACTION are similarly prepared. There is little point in the local authority imposing a RESTRAINT if no specification for its practical implementation is made available to departments and their business centres.

It may seem that the suggestion made earlier, (that Business Plans can be built from a departmental level), could create inconsistency and gaps, but our starting point was to take the MISSION STATEMENT and the CORE VALUES derived from it as an overall rubric for each department. So long as these CORE VALUES are at the heart of each department's Business Plan, then little difficulty should be experienced in ensuring consistency and cohesion between Business Plans of the respective departments of a local authority.

The PROCESS of PRODUCING the Business Plan is now complete.

There still remains, however, the need to

- **MONITOR, REPORT AND REVISE the plan from time to time;**

- **develop SERVICE LEVEL AGREEMENTS for the provision of inputs from other departments of the local authority;**

- **ensure that CASH FLOW is adequately secured;**

- **develop a MARKET STRATEGY for the business centre and/or department.**

SOME CHALLENGING QUESTIONS

1   Would your proposition, if carried through, promise benefits to the community?

If so what are these benefits and how do they meet the Council's objectives?

How will they be distributed and to whom and when would they accrue?

2   What disadvantages would you expect might flow from your work?

Who would experience them?

What, if any, remedies would correct them?

Is the technology for correcting them sufficiently advanced for the remedies to be available when the disadvantages begin to accrue?

3   What demands would the development of your proposition make upon resources of skilled staff, and are these resources likely to be available?

4   Is there a cheaper, simpler and less sophisticated way of achieving at least part of the proposition that you have in mind?

If so what would it be and what proportion of the total objective would have to be sacrificed if it was adopted?

5   What skills would be rendered obsolete by the development you propose and how serious a problem would the obsolescence of these skills create for the people who had them?

6   Is the work upon which you are engaged being done, or has it been done, or has it been started and stopped, in other authorities?

What experience is available from them that might help to assess this particular proposition?

7   If what you propose is not done, what disadvantages or penalties do you believe will accrue to the community and what alternative ideas might be considered?

8   If your proposition is accepted, what other work in the form of supporting systems should be set in hand simultaneously, either to cope with the consequences of it, or to prepare for the next stage and what would that next stage be?

9   If an initial decision to *proceed* is made, for how long will the option to stop remain open and how reversible will this decision be at progressive stages beyond that?

10   What are the resource implications of your proposition, compared with your projections?

8. Monitoring - Reporting - Revising

Producing a Business Plan will provide any organisation, whether an authority, a department or a business centre, with a considerable amount of work. This can clearly be seen from all that has already been described. In fact, it is recognised that this is of sufficient magnitude to promote feelings of "leaving well alone" and getting on with what might be considered as other more important priorities.

Nevertheless, it is our feeling that the preparation of a Business Plan has become a pre-requisite for any local government organisation that is required either to make a statutory rate of return on capital or to provide an efficient and effective service in the increasingly financially hostile environment.

However, once all the analysis and work has been done it must be appreciated that the finished plan is not a "bible" to refer to from time to time, and file away in the bookcase to gather dust. It is a living, breathing document to be used continually and altered to reflect changing circumstances and situations as and when they occur. It has another vital function in that it should be used to report to members and senior officers where the business is at, in comparison to where it should be, according to reasonable predictions. It will help the process of analysing why targets have not been met, or have been exceeded, and will need to be amended in the light of experience and altering situations.

What follow are our suggestions as to how the processes of monitoring, reporting and revising the Business Plan can be carried out in practical ways.

Objective Setting

The Business Plan will contain the agreed objectives, both primary and secondary. Some of these will be common to all or most business centres (eg to make a prescribed rate of return) and others will be specific to an individual business centre.

Members will have considered and agreed the overall objectives for the Department or DSO and the Chief Officers will be responsible for ensuring that these are achieved. In a large multi-disciplined department common in local government there will probably entail a process of "cascading" the objectives down into the organisation so that each business centre manager will be responsible for achieving the particular objectives in that area of work (eg the Building Manager is responsible through his/her supervisory staff, labour force and administrative support staff, for ensuring that the objectives of the Building Maintenance Section are fulfilled).

We believe that the objectives for a business centre should be discussed and agreed with that business centre manager and a timetable for achievement be set out over a reasonable period of time, say one year. The objectives need to list the actions necessary to achieve the required result and the stated performance indicators to be used to measure the success or otherwise of these actions.

A possible format indicating Secondary Objectives and Actions to be taken in the pursuit of Primary Objectives follows on the following three pages (Example 1)

EXAMPLE 1

TRANSPORT SECTION
OBJECTIVES YEAR 1

TRANSPORT MANAGER

(A)   To act as Authorised Officer in relation to the contract for the repair and maintenance of vehicle and plant.

Action

1.   Co-ordinate regular liaison and meetings with client/fleet managers to discuss and determine performance.

2.   Ensure through the Garage Supervisor that the fleet is maintained and/or repaired in accordance with the contract conditions.

3.   Liaise regularly with the section accountant to ensure that all appropriate income is being consistently recovered.

Success Criteria

The transport contract is operating to the satisfaction of fleet managers and achieving 5% rate of return on capital.

(B)   Oversee the day to day control and administration of the lease car fleet.

Action

1.   Daily contact with the Fleet Administrator to ensure that procedures and timescales are being adhered to.

2.   Regular monitoring to ensure that the Fleet Administrator and Service Supervisor are exchanging relevant information for the purpose of covering as much as possible of each other's jobs.

3.   Discussing and agreeing problems and/or policy changes as necessary with the Chief Officer.

Success Criteria

The leased car fleet is both managed and maintained to the satisfaction of lease car users and within the Council policies on this subject.

EXAMPLE 1 (CONT)

(C) **The parts store in the garage to be reorganised and proper stores charging procedures are in place.**

Action

1.   A full stock take and inspection of the parts store be undertaken within two months.

2.   Action taken to dispose of unwanted stocks etc within three months.

3.   Discussions take place with the Supplies Section to identify which stores could be kept centrally in future.

4.   Liaise with the Section Accountant to set up an appropriate stores recharging procedure within three months.

Success Criteria

(a)   The parts store is in a reasonable and tidy condition and   contains only those items which are relevant and appropriate.

(b)   A stores recharging procedure is installed.

(D) **Seek alternative location to deal with appropriate overspill work in the Garage.**

Action

1   Consider which activities could best be transferred to another location.

2.   Investigate alternative sites which might be capable of use.

3.   Carry out a feasibility study of any agreed location and make appropriate financial provision in next year's budget.

Success Criteria

More space is available for work in the garage by moving some work to another location within 15 months.

EXAMPLE 1 (CONT)

**(E)   Oversee the day to day control and administration of the
Health Service Contract.**

Action

1. Daily contact with the Garage Supervisor to ensure that
vehicles are being dealt with according to priorities.

2. Regular monitoring to ensure that repair information is
being recorded in accordance with Health Service
requirements.

3. Liaise regularly with the Section Accountant to ensure that
all appropriate income is being consistently recovered.

4. Regular liaison with the Health Service Engineer to ensure
that they are satisfied with the arrangements.

Success Criteria

The Health Service contract is managed to the satisfaction of
the Health Service and regular and appropriate income is
received as a result.

This procedure involves the particular manager and, by implication at least, the
business centre staff in the process of owning the business and accepting
responsibility for achieving the objectives in a reasonable time scale.

MONITORING

Previously we have described the process whereby objectives can be set out and
followed through by the managers and staff involved in the work. The importance
of this process and a commitment to it cannot be over stressed, for its success will
self evidently make the rest of the process that much easier.

However, it is necessary to have a formal but clear and simple method whereby
managers and their staff can follow progress (or lack of) and be involved as
appropriate in the monitoring process.

We suggest that each business centre objective, both primary and secondary,
that has been accepted and adopted should be listed in a bar chart format with
reference to the page number in the Business Plan which discusses the specific
objective.

Against each objective there needs to be a timetable over which the objective
can reasonably be reached. *A suggested format is set out opposite (Example 2).*

EXAMPLE 2

PURCHASING AND SUPPLY SECTION

PAGE	OBJECTIVE	YEAR 1 J F M A M J J A S O N D	YEAR 2 J F M A M J J A S O N D	YEAR 3 J F M A M J J A S
3.2	Replace computer system			
4.1(ii)	Move reception area			
	Provide new barrier control	COMPLETED		
5.1(i)	Appoint permanent purchaser	COMPLETED		
	Appoint permanent invoicer	COMPLETED		
7.6.4(i)	Flexible hours - investigate			
	Task training			
9.1(i)	Better trading statement	ONGOING		
12.10.5	Discuss stock levels with clients			
	every three months			

These objectives now become the working document of the business centre, with common goals that everyone in the section should be aware of and strive to attain.

During an agreed period (eg quarterly) the business centre manager should discuss the performance of the section with his/her senior manager and appropriate members of the section staff. They should agree whether targets have been achieved, and if not why and what corrective action should be taken over what timescale.

As a result of this process a new set of targets are established and agreed and the process starts on its next cycle.

The format set out on the previous page might now be modified to look like Example 3 on the opposite page.

EXAMPLE 3

PURCHASING AND SUPPLY SECTION

PAGE	OBJECTIVE	YEAR 1	YEAR 2	YEAR 3	Notes
3.2	Replace computer system				DELAYED PENDING OUTCOME OF BUILDING MAINT. CONTRACT
4.1(ii)	Move reception area				COMPLETED
	Provide new barrier control				WORK COMPLETED. AWAITING DECISION ON STAFFING.
7.6.4(i)	Flexible hours - investigate				TWO MONTHS TRIAL PERIOD BEING WORKED
"	Task training				TWO MONTHS TRIAL PERIOD BEING WORKED
9.1(i)	Better trading statement				NOT POSSIBLE AT THIS TIME
12.10.5	Discuss stock levels with clients every three months	ONGOING			
3.1	Improve purchasing arrangements for Highways materials		ONGOING		
6.3(1)	Method study of tasks in Supplies				

(Year 1, Year 2 each divided into quarters: JFM AMJ JAS OND; Year 3: JFM AMJ JAS)

REPORTING

Inevitably in local government there is a necessity for Members to undertake their responsibilities for ensuring that the objectives, which they have set, are being carried out and in accordance with any agreed timescales. The forum for dealing with this will vary between authorities, depending upon such matters as

- the degree of accountability,

- the ideological and political requirements of the authority, including possible formal union involvement,

- the size and position of the business centre in relation to the department.

Let us assume that there are at least two forums wherein the performance of the department or DSO is considered (in an appropriate committee or board of Members, and a union/management regular consultative meeting). It will be necessary to bring the performance of the department to them regularly say quarterly.

The bar chart set out in the previous section should be produced at these meetings. Each item shown should then be considered, and appropriate time given to resolving any difficulties and agreeing necessary modifications. After each meeting, the bar chart should be amended to reflect any agreed timetable changes or new objectives to be included.

This is obviously not an exhaustive process and, again depending upon local circumstances, there are other matters which can readily be reported upon without undue difficulty. In any case such matters should form the basic information which will be necessary to manage the business centre.

What we are here considering are such matters as

- monthly financial statements; *(see Example 4)*

- employment information or attendance summaries for the same period; *(see Example 5)*

- individual and ongoing sickness records which are beyond an acceptable "norm" and will require specific case work to be undertaken. *(see Example 6)*

EXAMPLE 4

ACCOUNTABLE DLO TRADING SUMMARY
TEN MONTHS PERIOD ENDING JANUARY YEAR 1   WEEKS IN MONTH = 4

	Cumulative to end of 9 months Year 1 £	Month 10 £	Cumulative to end of 10 months Year 1 £
Building Trades			
INCOME	2,228,006	297,204	2,525,210
COST			
Direct Labour	988,877	117,803	1,106,680
Vehicle and Plant	113,479	10,075	123,554
Materials	478,185	61,632	539,817
Other Direct Costs	62,018	7,230	69,248
Sub Total	**1,642,559**	**196,740**	**1,839,299**
Overheads	486,909	53,712	540,630
Return on Capital	31,091	3,109	34,200
Total Costs	**2,160,559**	**253,570**	**2,414,129**
SURPLUS	**67,447**	**43,634**	**111,081**

RESULTS BY COST CENTRE (Surplus in Brackets)

Direct Cost Accounts			
Area 1	(9,090)	(5,224)	(14,314)
Area 2	19,581	(904)	18,677
Area 3	(11,201)	(8,025)	(19,226)
Voids	(30,006)	(4,794)	(34,800)
RPTR	(14,418)	(3,954)	(18,372)
Painters	(8,214)	(2,457)	(10,671)
Drivers	(12,456)	(3,459)	(15,915)
Specialist Joinery	(12,228)	(2,187)	(14,415)
Window Fixing	(2,862)	(2,327)	(5,189)
Electricians	1,424	(353)	1,071
Emergencies	(14,612)	(3,400)	(18,012)
Sub Total	**(94,082)**	**(37,084)**	**(131,166)**
Overhead Accounts	26,635	(6,550)	20,085
SURPLUS	**(67,447)**	**(43,634)**	**(111,081)**

Rate of return at January Year 1 = 16%

EXAMPLE 5

EMPLOYMENT INFORMATION IN WORK HOURS AND EQUIVALENT FULL-TIME POSTS - MANUAL WORKERS
(EQUIVALENT FULL-TIME POSTS ARE SHOWN IN PARENTHESIS)

PERIOD FEBRUARY
4 WEEKS 20 WORKING DAYS

| CITY SERVICES (CONSTRUCTION SERVICES DIVISION) | ESTAB. WORKING HOURS THIS PERIOD | LOST TIME | | | | | | | | TOTAL AVAILABLE WORKING HOURS | OVER-TIME | TOTAL HOURS WORKED (EXCL. LOST TIME) | HOURS BELOW/ABOVE ESTAB. THIS PERIOD |
		LEAVE	SICK	YEARS RLLNG. AVGE.	TRAI-NING	ACT. SUP.	UNION	VACAN-CIES	TOTAL				
AREA 1 (19269)	1560 (10)	157 (1)	114 7%	660 3%	0	51	10	0 (0)	332 (2) 21%	1228 79%	708 (5) 45%	1936 (12) 124%	376 (2) 24%
AREA 2 (20679)	1560 (10)	82 (1)	140 9%	711 3%	64	156	0	0 (0)	442 (3) 28%	1118 72%	512 (3) 33%	1630 (10) 104%	70 (0) 4%
AREA 3 (32575)	2652 (17)	112 (1)	16 1%	124 4%	0	39	8	0 (0)	175 (1) 7%	2477 93%	199 (1) 8%	2676 (17) 101%	24 (0) 1%
P.T.R. (17153)	1248 (8)	100 (1)	141 10%	1438 8%	0	0	31	0 (0)	272 (2) 22%	976 78%	0 (0) 0%	976 (6) 78%	-272 (-2) -22%
VOIDS (17268)	1404 (9)	62 (0)	0 0%	154 1%	12	0	77	0 (0)	151 (1) 11%	1253 89%	559 (4) 40%	1812 (12) 129%	408 (3) 29%
PAINTERS (26685)	2184 (14)	71 (0)	104 5%	2403 9%	0	0	67	0 (0)	242 (2) 11%	1942 89%	150 (1) 7%	2092 (13) 96%	-92 (-1) -4%
BUILDING DRIVERS (6028)	468 (3)	15 (0)	8 2%	182 3%	41	0	2	0 (0)	66 (0) 14%	402 86%	47 (0) 10%	449 (3) 96%	-19 (0) -4%

139657 (TOTAL SECTION ROLLING AVG.) 6789   5% (SICK)

CITY SERVICES (CONSTRUCTION SERVICES DIVISION)	ESTAB. WORKING HOURS THIS PERIOD	LEAVE	SICK	YEARS RLLNG. AVGE.	TRAI-NING	ACT. SUP.	UNION	VACAN-CIES	TOTAL	TOTAL AVAILABLE WORKING HOURS	OVER-TIME	TOTAL HOURS WORKED (EXCL. LOST TIME)	HOURS BELOW/ABOVE ESTAB. THIS PERIOD
GRAFFITI SQUAD (4614)	468 (3)	23 (0)	8 2%	124 3%	0	0	0	0 (0)	31 (0) 7%	437 93%	0 (0) 0%	437 (3) 93%	-31 (0) -7%

EXAMPLE 6

MONTHLY(ACCOUNTING)SICKNESS RECORD FOR BUSINESS CENTRES.

DIVISION: CONSTRUCTION SERVICES   **PERIOD:** Say, 5 weeks

Section	Name	Hours	Weeks (in excess of 2 weeks)
Area 1	•••••• •••••• •••••• •••••• •••••• ••••••	18.25 24.50 70.00 31.00 16.50 23.00	2
Area 2	•••••• •••••• •••••• ••••••	28.00 16.00 4.00 31.00	 2 4
Area 3	•••••• •••••• •••••• ••••••	24.00 31.00 48.00 4.00	 2 3
Painters	•••••• •••••• •••••• •••••• •••••• •••••• •••••• •••••• ••••••	16.00 13.50 1.00 48.00 32.00 16.00 63.50 52.50	 2 2 33
Drivers	•••••• ••••••	39.00 29.00	

Notes: A procedure should be in place to deal with withose employees appearing in the last column (in excess of two weeks).

For example, those who reach 2 would be informally interviewed by their supervisor to identify any problems and consider reasons.

The employee on 4 would be formally interviewed in a structured process aimed at improving sickness records.

The employee on 33 could well be a long term sickness case where action is under way to retire on ill health grounds.

REVIEWING AND REVISING

We said earlier that the Business Plan should be a tool which is used by management and other concerned parties **as a guide to action**. In order for it to fulfil this essential function it will need to be revised significantly on a regular basis, probably and usually once a year. Earlier in this document we referred, when constructing the Business Plan of an existing business, to the analogy of the overhaul of a motor vehicle.

The process we now need to undertake using the same analogy could be compared with a yearly comprehensive service which should be carried out if the vehicle is to have a reasonable chance of running without major problems in the next year. There is no need here to "re-invent the wheel", as by and large the principal analyses have already been done.

We have found the layout in Example 7 to be a convenient and simple way of setting down the issues which have been agreed in the Business Plan.

At the annual review, each of the items would then be examined in turn and either modified, or rejected and replaced as appropriate. Necessary consideration should be given, and explanations of deviations from target should be discussed.

The lessons learnt from this exercise could then be shown as illustrated on Page 70 showing an example relating to Construction Services (Example 8)

In summary the Business Plan is an essential aid to running a successful business. The processes of objective setting, monitoring, reporting and revising are crucial if the plan is to be kept in a relevant condition and the business is to thrive. This chapter has explained these processes and outlined the methods that could be used to achieve the goals.

These are not prescriptive, and it is perfectly feasible and often desirable to adopt or modify these documents to meet local and individual needs.

What is of much greater importance is to ensure that some form of easily understandable system is in place in order to control the process of business planning.

EXAMPLE 7

BUSINESS PLAN
PRINTING SERVICES

Key Manager:
Main Product/Services:
Providing Printing and copying in-house in colour and black and white.
Booklet production perforating and numbering collating and folding

Key data	Prior Year 2	Prior Year 1
Employees	6 $^{1/2}$	6 $^{1/2}$
Expenditure	£210,330	£223,310
Income	£210,040	£225,027

Key Contracts	Supply Printing to value of £198,000. Photocopying to value of £53,000 to Council
Strengths	Strong customer base with the Council Local knowledge Committed workforce Geographical location
Weaknesses	Poor accommodation No computer system Old equipment Poor marketing
Competitors	Local printers (Frinter Print & Pica Ltd) Recent County buyout
Market size	Difficult to quantify but expanding as headteachers etc become cost centre managers
Market Development	Expand colour printing Expand photocopying Expand D T P and graphic design
Opportunities	Increase turnover by expanding into other areas Diversify eg microfilming
Threats	Competition from local printers Loss of DSOcontracts
Objectives	To provide printed matter at competitive market rates and an increase in turnover of 25% over the next five years
Strategies	Improved monitoring of cost. Expand our market
Key Actions	Lower prices to internal customers by increasing efficiency and turnover

Forecast

Year 1	Year 2	Year 3	Year 4	Year 5
£287,230	£301,590	£316,671	£332,500	£350,000

EXAMPLE 8

BUSINESS PLAN - YEAR 2 UPDATE

Division: Construction Services   **Manager:** . . . .
Section: Engineering
Main Services: Civil Engineering projects; Highways maintenance; Metalwork
construction; Electrical maintenance; Sewer maintenance; Sign
making; Emergency services

Key Data:	Year 1 (Forecast)	Year 1 (11 months position)	Year 2 (Forecast)
Employees:	50	57	60
Turnover:	£1.423M	£1.478M	£1.709M
Rate of Return:	5%	15%	5%

YEAR 1 PLAN REVIEW

	Actions	Targets	Achievements
1	Increase contract supervision by recruitment of an additional Agent.	Dec Year 1	Appointment made via promotion from workforce
2	Achieve more efficient site management by provision of on site accommodation and direct reporting to site.		Achieved on target.
3	Central purchase for on site deliveries.	Sept Year 1	More materials being delivered direct to site.
4	Seek improvements to downtime for repairs and servicing to vehicles and plant.	Dec Year 1	Transport section introduce extended day working in January. Downtime being reduced
5	Improvements to MOT by pre MOT checks taking place and parts needed purchased to reduce time off road.	Sept Year 1	Transport section introduction revised system for Year 2
6	When work offered customer to be given date of completion, advise of any delay and revised completion date.	Nov Year 1	Not implemented but system being investigated ready for Year 2

9. SERVICE LEVEL AGREEMENTS

It is remarkable that, though the topic of this book, "Business Planning" is clearly derived from the private sector, service level agreements in the practice of the private sector are not widely used.

Companies clearly make decisions as to whether they will provide support services on an in-house basis or a bought-in basis and if provided on the latter basis will arrange the usual form of business contract. If they make a decision to provide support services on an in-house basis then such support services, whatever the nature, will be regarded as an integral part of the operation.

CIPFA regards local authority current practice with regard to service level agreements to be in advance of developments in the private sector.

What we would argue however is that the private sector manager, as a natural part of managerial responsibilities, will have detailed and clear information on the inputs and associated costs necessary to provide the output - whether it be goods or services - of their own operational unit in line with the primary objectives of their enterprise and will have decided how best to acquire such support inputs.

Moreover, the lack of clarity that sometimes exists in many local authorities between PRIMARY OBJECTIVES, SECONDARY OBJECTIVES, RESTRAINTS and MEANS to achieve objectives, prevails to a somewhat lesser degree in the private sector organisation.

In particular, RESTRAINTS will have already been identified and challenged and the organisation will be operating with the bare minimum that it thinks appropriate. In the local authority sector where RESTRAINTS have been elevated accidentally or intentionally to the position of PRIMARY OBJECTIVES, the movement toward the establishment of service level agreements provides both operational and support services departments with the opportunity to clarify and challenge the conventional role of the centre of the organisation.

The driving forces towards the establishment of SLA's have manifestly been the changes in legislation

- on competition;

- on delegated finance to schools;

- on the ring-fencing of the housing revenue account;

- on the proposals on the provision of community care

- and the gearing effect of the introduction of community charge which itself has increased the political sensitivity of marginal spending decisions.

These changes have all forced the managers of operational units to question the role and value of central support departments. The paradox, of course, is that if one enters a SLA with a central support department one merely buttresses their traditional role as large, centrally controlling functions with an unhealthy pre-occupation with the minutiae of operational decision-making, thus damaging their ability to think strategically across the boundaries of the operational departments.

In the large, complex, multifunction, private sector organisation with which local authorities are sometimes compared, the support functions at the centre are very slim, dealing only with major cross-departmental strategies and policies and with the thinking through at a corporate level of new initiatives. In such organisations operational matters are provided for by qualified staff working on an in-house basis serving solely the needs of that department; a movement which is only slowly taking place in local government.

Were we to pursue the logic of Business Planning to the full, the operational departments would acquire whatever level of support skill they felt they required either within their own departments or by making contracts with external agencies.

We have however, to live with the reality of the foreseeable future and therefore, a finely-tuned SLA with whatever central support services the operational manager feels appropriate, becomes an essential lubricating mechanism to the effective working of an operational department, and so must become an integral part of its Business Plan.

The benefits of a SLA are usually summarised as follows:

- it makes **providers** more accountable for the quality and the costs of the services they deliver and encourages them to plan for the development of the service they offer

- it makes **providers** more responsible to the needs of the users

- it makes **users** more conscious of the costs of service from various types of supplier

- it makes **users** more concerned with monitoring the quantity and quality of the services they are paying for

- it makes **users** plan ahead for the support services they require and to make appropriate funding provision in their Business Plan.

The benefits are founded upon the belief that **users** will restrict consumption to accord with the value of the benefit received and to that which **their budget** can afford. From our discussion earlier in this chapter we would add that we believe a further benefit is the clarifying and questioning of OBJECTIVES, RESTRAINTS and MEANS which will ensue from consideration of a service level agreement with a view to lessening the cost burden upon the operational units in pursuit of their primary objectives.

For the authority as a corporate body there are, of course, some disadvantages. If **users** reduce their consumption of central support services, thereby leaving the centre with surplus capacity, there can be only three outcomes:

- selling spare capacity to external agencies

- spread the cost of spare capacity amongst existing users thereby increasing their costs.

- eliminate the spare capacity. (The restraint of a no-redundancy agreement could make this impossible).

Furthermore, there still exists the problem of how the central organisation copes with unexpected increases in demand. This is an especial difficulty if increased supply can only be provided in large increments eg a new mainframe computer. **Users** will wish to pay for their own increased demand but not capacity greater than they themselves require. In turn, central support **providers** are forced to create some kind of capital or reserve fund to cope with this contingency which will further increase the costs of their supply to **users**.

Similarly, **users** may be faced with an unpredictable upsurge in demand for this service without the funds/finance to meet the costs - **a classic way of alienating one's own clients/customers.**

Again a reserve/contingency fund to cope with this situation would seem a necessity, but financial regulations do not always make this an easy option.

Given the present situation it is imperative that operational departments forge an effective SLA between themselves and the supplier of their central support services so as to lubricate their provision of service to their customers.

Having examined a number of service level agreements for their effectiveness we would argue that they should contain the following features:

- the service to be provided

- the provider of the service

- the party paying for the service

- the charges to be made and the payment plan

- the period of the agreement

- the period of notice

- arrangements for monitoring and review

- the procedure for settling disputes

- the penalties for non-performance

- the help the user will provide and when

- the contact points for both parties

- the insurance liabilities of the respective parties

The provider will wish to make clear:

- the precise nature of the service to be provided

- limitations on the extent of service to be provided

- the quantity and quality of the service to be purchased

- optional services available on request

- procedure for variation

- response times

- method for dealing with inflation

A Service Level Agreement might look like Example 9 set out below:

EXAMPLE 9

A.   GENERAL

1.   This agreement is entered into between the Audit Service and the ─────────────────Department (hereinafter known as the Client Department). It takes effect on the 1st April, 19..... and covers the period to the 31st March, 19..... It may be renewed by an exchange of memoranda

2.   In this agreement the term "Minimum Audit Cover" (MAC) is defined as the annual amount of audit work based on a five year programme which the Head of Finance requires the Audit Service to provide in fulfilment of responsibilities under Section 151 of the Local Government Act 1972.

3.   Any matter which cannot be settled formally between the parties referred to in paragraph 1 above shall be referred to the Head of Finance. If either party is dissatisfied with the outcome they may appeal to the Chief Executive.

4.   This agreement may be varied by mutual agreement or by the direction of the Head of Finance at any time.

B.   SERVICES TO BE PROVIDED

The Services to be provided by this agreement shall comprise:-

1.   A programme of system reviews as agreed with the Head of Finance.

2.   A programme of compliance tests to confirm the correct operation of systems.

3.   Selective substantive testing as determined by the Chief Internal Auditor of areas needing further attention during compliance testing.

4.   The provision of advice on the interpretation and operation of financial practices and procedures as required.

EXAMPLE 9 (CONT)

5.   The initial examination of any alleged or suspected irregularity in order to provide the Client Department with advice on the further action to be taken.

6.   The above services shall be allocated as described in the Schedule of this agreement. (Not included).

C.   LIMITATIONS ON EXTENT OF SERVICE

1.   In the event of further audit work being required as a result of the initial examination of an alleged or suspected irregularity (see para B.5 above) the additional time will be the subject of a separate agreement with the Client department.

2.   Advice sought under paragraph B.4 above is limited to enquiries by telephone, memo, or letter. Advice requiring visits to establishments or provision of staff training shall be subject to separate agreement and charges.

3.   If the Chief Internal Auditor considers that the results of substantive testing reveal the need for further work which cannot be met from within the time allocated in this agreement he/she shall report the reasons to the Head of Finance who may, after consultation with the Client Department, direct that additional work is carried out at additional cost.

D.   AUDIT TIME AND CHARGES

1.   The Services described in Section B and the schedule to this agreement shall be provided to the Client Department by the allocation of ____ days audit.

2.   The charge for the services shall be an annual charge of £ _____ calculated at £ _____ per day.

3.   The charges stated in paragraph D.2 are fixed for the twelve months of this agreement ending 31st March Year 1. The rate for future years will be subject to agreement upon renewal of this agreement. The charges for any services agreed additional to this agreement shall be agreed at the time the additional services are contracted.

Example 9 (Cont)

4.   For the purposes of this agreement a day is defined as _____ hours being the "standard" day for Audit Staff. Clients should note that the time spent by audit staff on work for each client is recorded and the total divided by _____ hours to arrive at the number of productive days provided.

5.   Charges for services provided by this agreement will be payable by four quarterly payments of £___on the 15th Day of May, August, November and February.

E.   STAFF AND AUDIT ARRANGEMENTS

1.   The Chief Internal Auditor will assign staff to audit work in appropriate numbers and qualification to carry out the work described in paragraph C.1 and Schedule to this agreement.

2.   The Chief Internal Auditor will give the Client Department not less than 48 hours notice of the commencement of an audit. The Chief Internal Auditor may at his/her discretion commence an audit without notice if in his/her opinion the authenticity of financial records might be affected but must, if requested, supply the Chief Officer of the Client Department with the reasons for so doing within 48 hours of the commencement of the audit.

3.   If a Client Department is dissatisfied with the conduct or performance of an assigned member of staff, the Client Chief Officer shall report the matter to the Chief Internal Auditor who shall investigate the matter and report the action taken to the Chief Officer. If the matter cannot be resolved to the mutual satisfaction of both parties the matter shall be referred to Head of Finance.

A standard form for core service level agreement is set out as Example 10 overleaf. Examples 9 and 10 have been reproduced by kind permmission of CIPFA.

EXAMPLE 10

STANDARD FORM FOR CORE SERVICE LEVEL AGREEMENT

Agreement between _____

the _____ Department, Unit etc (the provider) and

the _____ Department, Unit etc (the user) for

services during the period _____ to_____

Specification

The services to be provided are described in the specification attached.

Charges

The provider will charge the user at the following rates

£ ____ per _____
£ ____ per _____
£ ____ per _____

plus £____ per _____ for any additional services requested which are not covered by the specification.

Inflation

The rates will be increased on each _____ in accordance with the _____ index.

The Facilities needed by the provider

The user agrees to give the provider the following information or documents at or before the times, and at the places, stated

Contact points for queries

Provider _____ (Phone_____)
User   _____ (Phone _____)

Method of Payment

The user will send a bill to the Head of Finance within _____ days of the end of each _____ and will send a copy at the same time to the user. The Head of Finance is asked to effect the charge in the accounts within _____ unless before then the user gives written notice (to both the provider and the Head of Finance) of an outstanding query.

Penalties

Charges will be reduced by £____ for each occasion on which _____ and by £ ____ for each_____._____

Arbitration

Disputes which the parties cannot resolve will be referred to the _____ for settlement.

Signed _____ Name _____ Title _____ Date _____

_____ Name _____ Title _____ Date _____

10. Cash Flow

Whilst in most of the private sector, the speed and volume of cash flow has a crucial part to play in the health of the business, in local government generally, little importance has yet to be attached to this vital function.

The traditional situation in local government has been the process whereby prime documents (eg time sheets, bonus records, stores requisitions, etc) of the "contracting" department are input through the Treasurers central accounting system, usually via a main frame computer. As a direct result, the "contracting" department is credited with the costs, and the "client" department's appropriate revenue account is debited with the same amount.

This system was an efficient and effective one, dealing with the "paper" transaction whilst giving the community value for money. It also generally ensured that "cash" flowed from the client to the contractor every time a prime document was input.

However, the onset of CCT and the resultant identification of separate client and contractor relationships has brought this previously effective system under scrutiny, particularly by client departments who feel the need to approve work before payment.

Furthermore, the necessity to seek work in a wider market also engenders its own problems. It is clear that any work carried out for an outside agency, whether in the public or private sector, will require the production of an invoice against which the customer can measure the service received and pay accordingly.

It is our opinion that, despite the increased costs involved in setting up an invoicing system, this should be done. All customers whether external or "in-house" should then be charged through the invoicing system; whether as a dedicated or "stand alone" departmental one, or as a development of the mainframe linked to the Council's accountancy system.

The introduction of an invoicing system will place a responsibility on all business centre managers and first line supervisors to ensure that **all work** including any variations from the agreed specification is identified and presented for the preparation of an invoice.

It cannot be over stressed that without the full commitment and participation of operational staff in this system, cash flow will become subject to large variations, giving a trickle of income most of the time, with subsequent spurts when concerted efforts are made to deal with the resultant problems caused by lack of income.

We have produced on the next page a checklist which should help business centre managers and supervisors to keep on top of this vital function.

CHECKLIST FOR BUSINESS CENTRE MANAGERS AND SUPERVISORS

a) Does the contract allow for interim payments?

b) Do you know the conditions attached to these?

c) Have you measured and checked <u>all</u> aspects of the work for the interim/final payment?

d)   Where there are no formal contract conditions, do you have a system for checking and measuring the work for claiming income?

e)   When you have carried out work for other departments, particularly small, irregular, casual jobs, do you ensure that claims are being made for payment?

f)   Have you provided all information, and details of your customer to the accountant/administrator sending the accounts?

g)   Do you have a system for ensuring that the invoice has been sent?

Remember Accountants are not magicians and Administrators are not mind readers. It is **your** responsibility to ensure that work is measured; that all relevant information is passed for the invoice to be sent; and that checks are made to ensure that this has been done.

Cash flow is vital to *your* business; it is *your* income to be recovered and therefore *your* problem if it is not regularly maintained.

11. MARKET AND MARKET STRATEGY

"Marketing" and a market strategy are key elements in planning for a successful future for a department or business centre. It is a task that needs to be carried out when drawing up on overall Business Plan and the supporting business plans for each area of operation.

In the commercial sector, a well planned enterprise does not think of moving forward without a considered market strategy, and is unlikely to receive financial backing without such a strategy in evidence.

Although most of local government is relatively new to the commercial market place, virtually all DSO business areas are either already subject to competition or will be by 1992. Similarly, the likely private sector competitors are also relatively new to dealing with public sector business on such a large scale.

This situation is without precedent and therefore established commercial marketing techniques can only go part way to helping find a place in the market. However, the commercial sector has a largely successful track record in marketing and we believe the way forward is to adapt the techniques already available to suit local government needs. This will provide a model for the new market and the pioneering work required will bring the benefits that the commitment and effort deserves.

How do we actually go about achieving a market strategy? Firstly there are two important definitions which need to be understood in the case of the first, and decided upon in the case of the second.

> **McDonald's definition** - The management process of identifying, anticipating and satisfying customer requirements profitably.

> **Business definition** - The definition must be in terms of customer need or benefit and not in terms of product or production capability. Therefore, what a business thinks it is producing is not of first importance - especially not to the future of the business and to its success - what the customer thinks he/she is buying, what he/she considers value, is decisive.

Success depends upon a thorough understanding of the market and its customers.

We have already identified the principal determining factors in Chapter 6, and overleaf outline a checklist of practical tasks to be undertaken to focus the mind on the fundamental question "What business are we in?"

CHECKLIST OF TASKS

MARKET ANALYSIS AND RESEARCH
Customer Analysis

(a)   What is the customer paying for (or getting)? - benefit/s perceived and value?

(b)   Why is the customer buying? - is it quality, service, value, reliability, status and price or a combination of these?

(c)   What do customers expect? - is it price, quality, service or all?

(d)   How is the customer buying? - frequency etc.

(e)   When is the customer buying? - seasonal, particular events, regular/repeats

(f)   Who is the customer? - Council, private etc. - include potential customers

To back up this section, in the ideal world, a full customer (client) survey would be undertaken to obtain detailed analysis on their views.

MARKET MEASUREMENT
Information needed on potential market share.

(a)   Size of market (volume and value if available)?

(b)   Trends - is market growing, declining, stable?

(c)   Market share - who are the competitors? What do you know about them?

(d)   Seasonality - how can the effects be minimised?

Also need to consider:-

(a)   What customers say

(b)   What customers do

(c)   What customers have done

COMPETITIVE ANALYSIS

(a)   Identify existing and potential competitors direct and indirect - strengths and weaknesses - describe them.

(b)   Analyse competitive position, ie market share and segments.

(c)   What is the ability of new entrants to enter the market?

(d)   What is the bargaining power of customers?

(e)   Evaluate existing resources (capacity) and existing marketing performance.

(f)   What do customers think of them?

MARKETING DECISIONS
Segmenting the Market

Customer Based

(a)   Customer needs and preferences - perceived benefits.

(b)   Define purchase and service use behaviour.

(c)   What are customer characteristics?

Business Based - Is it

(a)   Mass market - address total market with one programme. Requires large number of customers with similar requirements.

(b)   Niche - Select single segment which represents the possibility of building a defensive position against competition.

(c)   Multi-Niche - Selection of several segments offering different products and/or services.

Market Positioning

(a)   What are customer purchase criteria?

(b)   What are customer preferences?

(c)   What are customer perceptions of competitive services or products?

(d)   Do you need to introduce new products?

(e)   Do you need to alter perception of existing service and/or product?

(f)   Do you need to alter customer's perceptions?

Service/Product Strategy

(a)   Branding - do you need to differentiate product/service from competitors through name, design feature etc.?

(b)   Does your service/product have a life cycle, if so where are you/ it currently?

Pricing Strategy - To have a pricing policy you need to know

(a)   Business costs

(b)   Demand for service/product

(c)   Profit objective

(d)   Is customer price conscious/aware/sensitive?

Sales Plan

(1)   *Promotion Strategy*

Components include Advertising, Public Relations, Publicity and Promotions

(a)   Select target audience i.e. mailing list - who to include.

(b)   Determine objective

(c)   Select appropriate message

(d)   Describe approach to be adopted to create customer awareness.

(2)   *Distribution and After Sales Strategy*

(a)   What methods to be used to get service/product to customer in a manner that suits the customer.

(b)   After sales service - if relevant indicate the importance of this in customers purchasing decision and how commitments will be met.

(c)   Compare your after sales service with competitors and highlight advantages/disadvantages over competitors.

ESTIMATED MARKET SHARE

1.   Summarise features of service or product which will enable it to succeed in the face of existing and potential competition.

2.   Highlight customers who have made or are prepared to make purchase commitments and indicate future major customers and why they will become so.

Based on the foregoing there is a significant amount of research and evaluation to be undertaken by each business area. There will be a variety of different answers given the diversity of the business activities and some aspects of the checklist may not be relevant.

However, the issues which the questions raise and the answers obtained will be of significant help in producing a market strategy for the department or business centre.

Three final points on marketing. Firstly, although some departments of some authorities may be large enough to directly employ marketing specialists (eg Leisure Services) many will realise that the cost of doing so is out of proportion to their business.

From experience we would say that marketing is, or should be, a line management function, and staff at all managerial levels within the business centre should be charged with that responsibility.

This leads to our second point. Marketing theory is a specialist subject with a plethora of information and training packages available.

It has again been our experience that it can provide a rewarding pay-off for the business to set up "in house" training for relevant managerial and supervisory staff. This is likely to engender an awareness of the need to be market orientated and to instil the requirement into the culture of the business.

Thirdly, it will be necessary to set up some form of marketing database, either manual or computer based, depending on the size of the business, and to ensure that this is constantly updated and relevant. The wider the range of customers the greater the requirement to keep accurate information about them. This is self evident in the commercial world but for most in local government it is a point which until now has generally not arisen.

We set out overleaf components of a marketing information system, and would offer the following quotation as closing words both to this chapter and to Part I of this book.

> **"The purpose of the business is to get and keep a customer. Without customers, no amount of engineering, wizardry and clever financing or operations expertise, can keep the company going. To do well, what should not be done is to do badly"**
>
> *Theodore Levitt*
> *The Marketing Imagination*

Part II of the book sets out examples of the practical applications of Business Planning and marketing in the services of Building Maintenance and Printing.

COMPONENTS OF A MARKETING INFORMATION SYSTEM

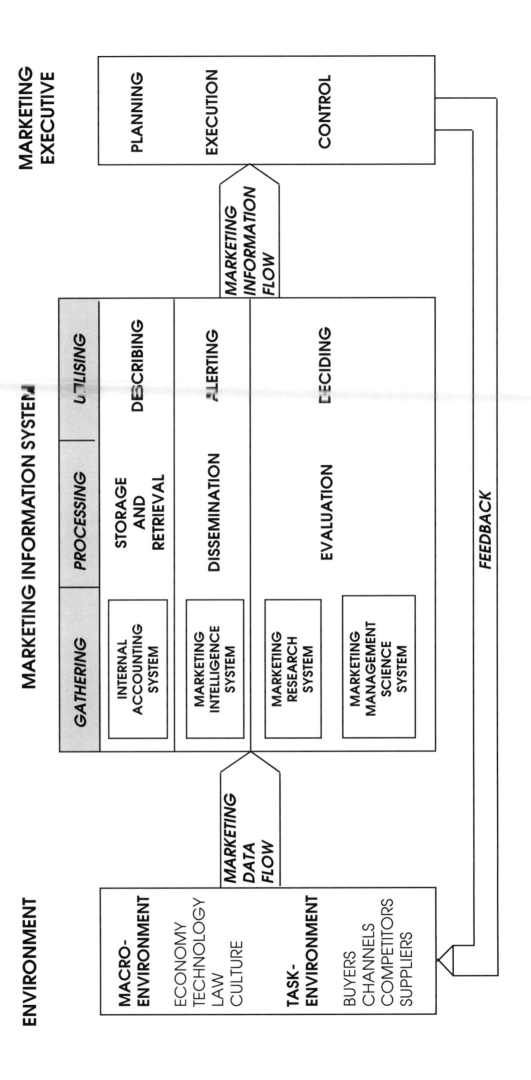

ENVIRONMENT

MARKETING INFORMATION SYSTEM

MARKETING EXECUTIVE

GATHERING	PROCESSING	UTILISING
INTERNAL ACCOUNTING SYSTEM	STORAGE AND RETRIEVAL	DESCRIBING
MARKETING INTELLIGENCE SYSTEM	DISSEMINATION	ALERTING
MARKETING RESEARCH SYSTEM	EVALUATION	DECIDING
MARKETING MANAGEMENT SCIENCE SYSTEM		

MACRO-ENVIRONMENT
ECONOMY
TECHNOLOGY
LAW
CULTURE

TASK-ENVIRONMENT
BUYERS
CHANNELS
COMPETITORS
SUPPLIERS

MARKETING DATA FLOW

MARKETING INFORMATION FLOW

PLANNING

EXECUTION

CONTROL

FEEDBACK

Redrawn from Kotler (1972) p.295 and reproduced by kind permission of Marketing Decisions

PART II

THE APPLICATIONS

PREFACE TO PART II

The remainder of the book is devoted to examples of the practical applications of both Business Planning and the development of Market Strategies.

In order to provide as wide an illustration as possible within the limits of this publication, we have used examples taken from an "acountable" area of work under the compulsory competition regulations (Building Maintenanoo) and a typical support service (Printing), which is also likely to be subject to CCT in the foreseeable future.

They are examples firstly of a very lengthy and detailed analysis of a business area, and then of a comparatively brief but sharpened version for a different service. We do not recommend one in favour of the other, but leave it to the reader to consider the appropriateness of each.

There are, of course, alternative methods of interpretation of the processes which would be acceptable in differing circumstances.

1. Business Plan - Building Maintenance

1. Introduction

The business consists of - Carpentry; Plumbing; Bricklaying and associated wet trades; Painting; Glazing; Electrical and Engineering Skills.

These skills are combined together to provide a building maintenance service to the Housing Department and other clients.

We are good at providing an all round building maintenance service. It can be said that some parts are more profitable than others. However, **what is our business?** It is one of providing a complete service; therefore the business must be looked at in overall terms.

The less profitable areas enable the more profitable areas to exist and make those higher profits. To cut the less profitable areas adrift would be dangerous.

2. Objectives

2.1　To meet the rate of return target for the Building Maintenance section required under the 1980 Planning and Land Act. (PRIMARY)

2.2　To win the five year Housing Schedule of Rates contract. (SECONDARY)

2.3　To improve the competitiveness of uPVC window production by the introduction of our own glass making facility. (SECONDARY)

3. Productivity and Operational Methods

3.1　Productivity

We regularly have production information which indicates that productivity is good within the present system. Therefore we could say that productivity is good. However, the system measures all work done rather than just chargeable work done. Therefore there is an incentive to use the easiest solution to generate an individual payment.

The measurement system is precise, ie it evaluates particular jobs accurately within a specified set of circumstances. However, the nature of the work means that there is a wide variation in circumstances for the same job (it is not a production line); consequently targets "age" and the precision is lost.

Productivity against chargeable work can be improved by directing the effort towards making only these items generate income. This would probably raise productivity by 10% to 20%.

The administration cost of the bonus system is also significant, particularly with the manual systems used at the moment.

A major saving in these costs could be achieved by simplifying the method of payment and computerising the process. It is estimated that up to two bonus administration jobs could be saved, generating a saving in the order of £20,000 per annum in this function.

Action: Change incentive scheme to be more tender led and reduce administration cost.

Target Date: End Year 2

3.2 Working Methods

(A)   At the present time work is split on a trade basis in most cases. This is perfectly acceptable where a job is split totally across that trade. Problems have tended to arise where there has been a need for multi trade working, with the ticket being passed from one section manager to the next with inevitable delays, however small. At the same time no particular person is responsible for that job. It is desirable that one section manager organises the work and directs all the resources. To overcome this problem the section workload should be split on an area basis where jobbing is concerned, or on a contract basis where programmed work is concerned. This provides accountability for each job.

It will be necessary to split the City up into areas. It is quite clear that if workload is short in one area the workload should be transferred from other sections. There must not be a fixed dividing line which people cannot cross.

Each section manager should be responsible for 12 to 20 employees of varying trades. Teams can then be established to carry out the installation of baths, kitchens and other multi trade jobs from within the group as and when needed.

The administration of these teams will be carried out by a support officer who will calculate bonus, help plan work and submit invoices and liaise with the Surveying Department.

This will hopefully develop a more closely knit team with the administration and work being in one unit rather than being divorced as it is presently. To maintain consistency across the teams there is a need to have an overall control for the sorting out of problems and dissemination of information. This would be carried out by the Contracts Manager.

Action: Design organisation chart to suit operational methods.

Target Date: September Year 1

(B)   Radio communications need to be improved so that people can be directed more easily to jobs, and problems resolved without having to return to the yard every time. We have a limited radio communication system at the moment - it would be prudent to extend this system to all vehicles in time. This again should add to our flexibility.

Action: Introduce better radio communications.

Target Date: End of Year 3

(C)   The collection and delivery of materials to and from sites is difficult and presently requires three lorries. Although every effort is made to maximise loads our policy to remove waste within 24 hours means that sometimes small loads are carried. There is a need to investigate other forms of collection and delivery, eg demountable bodies or skips to see if there are any advantages.

Action: Review delivery and collection of materials.

Target: December Year 2

3.3 Productivity Information

Production information is produced regularly by the work planning office. This shows the performance level for each group. This information is reasonable. It is, however, related to the present bonus system and as this changes the information will have to change to suit.

Action: Redesign production information in line with progression, changing the bonus scheme.

Target Date: End Year 2

4. COSTS
4.1 General

Efficiency is making best use of all the resources thereby controlling unit costs. Areas affecting efficiency are -

- Information systems to show what we are achieving and whether we are meeting the targets we are setting ourselves.

- Plant utilisation

- Material wastage

- Overhead costs

- Making sure we get paid for the job

- Ensuring there is enough workload

- Flexibility

- Training

(A) Information systems

The present information systems are fairly crude and only give general information which makes managing imprecise. We receive information on the following:

- Plant utilisation carried out by the section manager.

- There is no information on material usage - there has been no need to date, the client has paid without question.

- Overhead costs are monitored through the costing system although this needs improving to give more detailed information.

- The Quantity Surveyor and Accountant have set up systems to make sure we get paid for the job.

- Ensuring we have enough workload and planning that work is carried out manually

This is cumbersome when dealing with 35,000 job tickets per annum. Inevitably tickets get lost and priorities are missed. A computerised system is needed to monitor this.

To enable us to take any action on the other factors affecting efficiency we need reliable information otherwise we might make invalid judgements, or expand effort for very little reward.

Action: Review information systems and improve or change present systems to give meaningful detailed information.

Target Date: End Year 2

(B)   Staff Retention and Recruitment

The operational staffing levels are shown on the table below

	Prior Year 2	Prior Year 1	Year 1	Year 2 (Projected)
Bricklayers	20	18	16	18
Carpenters	24	25	26	26
Painters	18	12	10	10
Plumbers	15	18	16	16
Drivers	3	3	4	4
SUB TOTAL	80	76	72	74
uPVC Fixers	0	0	10	12
uPVC Factory	0	2	10	12
Woodmill	6	7	8	8
SUB TOTAL	6	9	28	32
TOTAL	**86**	**85**	**100**	**106**
STAFF TURNOVER	**N/A**	**N/A**	**37%**	

It can be seen from the table that we have a fairly high turnover of staff. We have also found it difficult to attract sfaff particularly in the area of skilled trade operatives (carpenters, bricklayers and plumbers etc.). The table below shows the operational staff age profile. It can be seen that it is generally a young workforce which might mean they are possibly more mobile between employers.

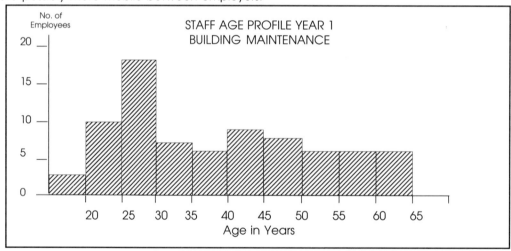

To attract and retain a skilled workforce we need to ensure that we pay a market rate which can be anything between £200 and £350 per week at the present time. However, these wages are generally paid on goods produced rather than on a time basis. We are fairly confident that our prices overall are realistic; therefore to generate more income to individuals, production will need to rise.

There is·a practical upper limit at the present time on earnings of £250, this includes bonus and overtime. Although there is an earning differential it must also be recognised that the organisation does give benefits through better working conditions, eg sickness pay, holiday pay and the provision of protective clothing etc. Obviously the benefits of these vary from individual to individual depending on the use made by each, but an evaluation of these shows that they are worth between £20 and £40 per week. This puts the earning level toward the middle of the band.

Increased earning must be achieved by increased productivity. The present method of bonus payment is restrictive in that there is an imposed ceiling. This needs to be removed and replaced by the freedom to earn against production. Therefore the bonus schemes need reviewing to become tender led but allowing the operative to earn more for more production.

Any incentive scheme can lead to a lowering of standards - this must not be allowed to happen and penalties must be used to avoid this situation.

Action: Review payment schemes to become more tender lead and provide a package that will attract and retain staff.

Target Date: December Year 2

(C)   Holidays

Each section manager is responsible for the planning of that section's holidays. This appears to work reasonably well at present time. The only problems that occur are around the end of the year when holiday has to be taken. More flexibility is required with holidays, so that they can be carried over or perhaps bought out.

Action: Negotiate with staff ways around holiday build up at the end of the year to achieve more even holiday usage.

Target Date: End Year1

(D)   Sickness

Section	Prior Year 2 %	Prior Year 1 %	Year 1 %	Year 2 % (Projected)
Plumbers	4	8	7	
Bricklayers	3	3	9	
Carpenters	6	6	6	
Painters	7	6	11	
Drivers	6	1	1	
Average	5	5	7	5

The sickness record as shown above is reasonable. It will be monitored monthly and anyone exceeding a specific level will be interviewed to establish a cause and to see if the situation can be improved. A sickness level of 5% is built into the labour rates. 5% is the accepted norm within the industry and is our target figure.

Action: To constantly review sickness and absence levels.

Target: Ongoing.

(E)   Materials

On the small jobbing work it is difficult to isolate wastage within any particular job. Again the financial reports should show the material cost situation overall and again it is up to the section manager to reduce wastage by managing to an absolute minimum.

On programmed, more long term work wastage on particular work can be isolated to particular areas and a regular check maintained. This needs to be done through the job costing system so that questions are regularly asked and again the section manager made aware and asked to review it.

Action: Monitor material costs against the tender and carry out such actions as necessary.

Target Date: Ongoing

(F)   Transport

(i)   This is a difficult area within the building maintenance section as the vehicle is really a mobile storage facility as well as for materials handling. The section managers now monitor their vehicles monthly, and they are aware of the costs. It is up to them to utilise them in the best possible manner. These reports are subject to scrutiny and raise questions which hopefully will develop awareness with the section managers.

Action: Monitor transport utilisation weekly.

Target Date: Ongoing

(ii)   We presently run a fleet of mainly Sherpa vans up to six years old. The annual cost for running these vehicles (including fuel) is £2850 on average per vehicle.

The vehicles themselves are not ideal for the job they are doing in that the bodies are too narrow. We have recently investigated other alternatives and have decided that the Ford Transit range with its wider bodies and side opening doors best meet our requirements. The present fleet will take years to replace under the existing arrangements. The present fleet mostly runs on leaded fuel and cannot be changed to run on unleaded.

We have investigated a lease hire arrangement within the leasing scheme and it would appear that Ford Transit vans can be provided at around £2000 per annum, on a three year lease, excluding fuel. Fuel costs are approximately £500 per annum. Each vehicle would need racking out, which is estimated in the order of £300 per vehicle. So this should represent an estimated saving of £550 per vehicle over the three year period. It would provide a new fleet, giving the organisation a better image and also allowing us to move to unleaded fuel at an earlier time by changing a large number of our vehicles now instead of over the next three years. As the remaining vehicles reach three years of age, consideration should be given to lease hire versus purchase at that time.

Action: Review transport needs, evaluate lease hire situation and change vehicles accordingly.

Target Date: December Year 1

(iii)   The building vehicle fleet is serviced and maintained by the DSO workshop. Presently vehicles can be delayed in servicing or during repair for no apparent reason, adding extra cost to the running of the overall fleet.

A new relationship must be built up with the garage and better communication established so that the vehicles are out of action for the least possible time.

Action: Negotiate improved servicing and repair procedure with the garage.

Target Date: End Year 1

5. ADMINISTRATION AND OVERHEADS

5.1 Control

Overheads are set up as a separate cost centre. This will be reviewed at each period and investigated accordingly.

Action: Monitor overheads against target in tender.

Target Date: Ongoing

5.2 Council Policies

Council policies per se do not hinder the DSO. In fact they generally support and help us. The major concern, however, is that when policy is introduced it is done without due regard to our culture. In most cases it is possible to adapt most policies to our particular culture. However, this should be thought through at the outset rather than at a later stage when the policy is in place.

Perhaps the most quoted example is the equal opportunities policy and its delaying effect on employment. The policy in itself is admirable and should be of great benefit to the organisation in getting the right person for the job. However, initially the system imposed a four to six week delay on an appointment from advertising to employment. This was unacceptable as replacement of people is needed generally in a two to three week period after the post falls vacant because of workload considerations. This imposed delay creates resentment towards the policy. Instead of being considered a "good thing" it becomes a "bad thing" and the result is the policy is viewed as no good, or as "interfering" by the people who have to work with it.

The details and implications at department level of any new central policy need to be thought through before their introduction. That does not mean to say that objections should not be over-ridden; it is just important to understand the detail of those objections and what difficulties they might make.

The other problem area has been the speed at which decisions are needed. Problems arise and some need very quick responses. Take tendering as an example. A tender can be announced and need to be returned within a six week period - well within the pattern of committee cycles. Decisions may be needed that are fundamental to the organisation. This is not possible under normal committee patterns. The introduction of the Direct Services Board with its fuller powers should hopefully mitigate this situation.

5.3 Support Services

It is important that Support Services do in fact support the DSO and not the DSO support the Support Services. However, for this to happen the DSO needs to know what it wants. Here is the first dilemma. For the DSO to know what it wants it needs expert advice, and it is forced into the arms of the Support Services for this. Do we trust them to give us this advice without bringing in other considerations of corporate policy and therefore giving unoriginal advice.

We need from Support Services the best solution to the problem for the DSO. It is then up to the DSO to present this case. Support Services should not be looking over their shoulder to see what is happening elsewhere.

They should recognise this and proffer advice but it is not their job to say. "no you cannot do this," either. This situation prevails to an extent with Personnel and ITS at the present time, and it must be purged so that the DSO can move forward unencumbered by this centralised view.

What does the Building Maintenance need immediately from Support Services?

> 1. Information needs are growing and we can no longer operate on the simple system we have. We need more accurate information more regularly. Do we need our own computer specialist?

> 2. Personnel needs - we need someone who is dedicated to the DSO at a fairly high level who understands the detail of our organisation and can react authoritatively to new initiative/policies, putting the clear implications of such a policy on the DSO into the debate.

Action: Review need for expert advice from Personnel and ITS, and how that advice should be given, whether centrally or from within the DSO.

Target Date: Mid Year 2

6.   RETURN ON CAPITAL

This has been dealt with under the volume of business in paragraph 10.

7.   EFFECTIVENESS

Do we know what our clients think about our effectiveness?

This is an area of conflicting perceptions even from the same individuals. There appears to be a general feeling from Housing Repairs and Maintenance that we do a good job and are thoughtful and caring towards the tenants. However, in the same breath we can be accused of not being organised to carry out jobs, particularly where more than one trade is involved, and they therefore prefer to use others.

The imposition of the DSO and the political support for the organisation is seen as a constraint on the individual housing officer in freedom to act and get the best value for money. This creates a confusing set of criteria where the housing surveyor is told to get the best value for money and at the same time is being coerced into using the DSO whatever the cost. We therefore become dominant instead of an equal. There is a need to get across that the schedule of rates is not a shopping list. It is a priced document to cover all eventualities - some items will be expensive, some will be cheaper, but the document generates income in total not just from particular items.

Housing have a number of works budgets not all coming from the one source. Not all of the housing clients are aware of what we can do. This also applies to Architects and other departments. We have relied too much on being a passive receiver of work rather than an active chaser.

There is a constant need to let people know we exist and what we can do, and for us to find out what is likely to happen so that we can influence decisions at the earliest moment.

We now have a growing number of external customers and the feedback from these areas is good. For example, the hospital positively state that they prefer us to win their contracts. We provide a full service and are confident that we charge a reasonable price. The difference here is that we are in a completely formal relationship where the rules are clear and everybody is sure where they stand - problems are resolved amicably without people looking over their shoulders.

The DSO needs to treat its in-house clients with respect and we need to demonstrate that they are important and we should not expect work as of right because we are the same body.

How can we get improved feed back?

True feed back can only occur where there is a measure of trust and understanding with no one party dominant. This is clearly happening where we deal with outside bodies. It is not the case internally where pressures from both sides and "corporate views" create barriers.

However, it is imperative that we achieve what the client wants so the barriers have to be broken, and real trust developed. To do this more time will need to be put aside for meeting the client both formally and informally. The information from these meetings will be analysed for common themes and this information acted upon and passed to all members of the organisation. It is also important that we are able to pass criticism back to the client without repercussion so that they can use the information. There should be one aim - that the working of the contract is improved to everyone's advantage.

Action: Promote and market organisation to internal and outside customers. Provide the staff resources to carry this out.

Target Date: September Year 1

8. INFORMATION

We receive regular business centre information which shows the overall position. We are, however, unable to analyse this information in any great detail. We are unable to obtain access to actual costs and income on a particular job. The system only accounts for costs as they are paid. This is alright for payroll and stores issues, but for materials supplied directly to a job it could mean that costs could be as much as three months behind. There is a need to change the system to commitment costing.

We need the facility to look at the actual position on any particular job on a regular basis. This will become more acute as the number of customers rises. It is important that we see the effect of different charging strategies. This enables decisions to be made on future contracts. We also need more management information on progress. We are unable to obtain any up to date information on outstanding jobs at the present time.

We need consistent up to date information regularly. We need the facility to be able to manipulate this information into various forms so that particular analysis can be carried out. For example, what is the frequency of worktype from the schedule of rates? Where is work located in the City? What is an average response time?

Action: Review information needs and prepare new management systems.

Target Date: End Year 2

9. ORGANISATION

Our organisation needs to be flexible to meet the needs of our varying customers, and get the most efficient solution to every problem.

Action: Structure organisation so that supervision is directed towards individual section managers responsibilities for individual jobs.

Target Date: September Year 1

10. VOLUME OF BUSINESS

10.1 Turnover - Rate of Return

The actual turnover, profit and rate of return are listed below for the previous four years:-

	Turnover	Profit	Rate of Return
Prior Year 3	£1,905,000	£149,600	27%
Prior Year 2	£2,129,000	£141,700	24%
Prior Year 1	£2,280,000	£102,800	15%
Year 1	£2,650,000	£159,000	20%

Our profits target has been to achieve 5% rate of return on assets because it has been the intention of the organisation to allow our internal clients to use their money for their service rather than provide excessive profits for the DSO. Do we take this view for the future? Do we set our sights higher? Aiming at 5% allows us to stay in business but not to develop. For Year 2 and Year 3, this level has already been set in the Building Maintenance schedule of rates. However, should we look for higher target margins in other tenders?

Do we take as much as we can from the market place or do we take a consistent margin? We should take the view that we will take what the market can stand because winning tenders does not guarantee everything will go right every time. Therefore we must get to know the market by regularly tendering, and price accordingly.

Accordingly our objective should be to make 5% rate of return on schedule of rates work and what the market will stand on other contracts (internal and external). Our minimum target rate of return is projected at 5%.

Our projected profit margins are laid out below:-

	Turnover	Profit	Rate of Return
Year 2	£2,800,000	£42,000	5%
Year 3	£3,010,000	£44,000	5%
Year 4	£3,250,000	£49,000	5%
Year 5	£3,480,000	£52,000	5%
Year 6	£3,740,000	£56,000	5%

For Years 2 and 3 we have an assured workload and we experienced very little competition on the schedule of rates. We believe the market is going to get tighter over the next two years - builders are already having to discount new build, and land prices are holding. This will mean that contractors will need to look elsewhere for their workload.

There has been a growth in small specialist building firms in line with the growth of the industry and they will initially be cutting margins before any shake out. There appears to be a growth in building maintenance contractors as government organisations, larger companies and other institutions contract out particular functions rather than carry them out in-house. This means that there will be a growth in potential market but also a growth in real competitiors.

The in-house workload is under threat from a government determined to relieve local authorities of their raison d'être. Other building work (office blocks etc) will probably slow down. Consequently such healthy profit margins are not predicted as previously, with them being closer to the required rate of return. It is also of concern that turnover will be difficult to increase beyond general levels of inflation, within day to day maintenance. However, it should be possible to expand turnover by looking at specialist areas (see paragraph 13).

11. WHAT ARE THE THREATS AND RESTRAINTS?

11.1 The Law

- Goods and Services Act 1970

- Local Government Planning & Land Act 1980

- Local Government Act 1988

- Right to Buy

- Pick a Landlord

11.2 Government Policies/Perceptions

a) Central Government financial policies are reducing financial support to local government.

b) The general attitude of the present Government towards local authority controls.

c) The perception that private sector management must be better than public sector management.

The law and Government policies certainly restrict our market and do not give us equality of opportunity with our competitors.

The general thrust towards putting out to competition all local government functions will affect our clients, certainly in the next five to seven years if this Government stays in power. This willl mean that our clients will be competing to stay in business as well as ourselves, which is certainly going to have its effect on us when everyone will be directed to winning their business and not dealing with us.

However, within the framework of the law there are a large number of potential customers and a significant amount of work. One advantage of these customers is that they are public sector and feel under the same threats as ourselves. Therefore they are sympathetic and understanding of our problems and consequently biased towards us. This is an advantage and must be exploited for all it is worth.

12. HOW COMPETITIVE ARE WE?

We have never been tested directly on the schedule of rates for our largest contract. The only measure we have is against standard prices gathered together by other agencies. When judged against these criteria we would appear to be competitive. It is difficult to measure against this information however as we are not sure as to whether it was produced on a "like for like" basis.

We have recently started competing for individual contracts up to £400,000 in value and meeting the market; winning by margins of only 2% to 3%. This leaves very little room for error and means that we will inevitably lose some as other contractors get to know the market, with us in it.

13. How can we increase Market Share?

At the moment 90% of our workload comes from the Housing Department. We have already decided this workload is under threat and is likely to decrease rather than increase. We need therefore to seek out other work from outside customers.

We have the expertise to carry out building maintenance and small work contracts. This has been carried out for the housing client for many years fairly successfully. However, there has been no positive drive to expand the workload beyond this client. Other clients have come to us because they have heard of us. Even clients within the Housing Department do not use us automatically.

There is a need to convert this potential market into work by telling people about ourselves. This extends outside the authority to other authorities and public bodies. We have identified through the marketing strategy a possible £5 million additional workload. *How do we convert that into real work?*

Action
>   *(1) Identify new clients and get on the tender list.*
>   *(2) Tender for it and win it.*
>   *(3) Provide sufficient resources to be able to do it.*

Commencement Target Date: September Year 1

Listed below are our customers and prospective customers:-

EXISTING
City Council
>   Housing Repair and Maintenance
>   Housing Estates
>   Estates
>   Architects
>   Engineering
>   Environmental Health
>   Leisure
>   DSO

County Council
Health Authority
Housing Associations
Housing Societies
General Public
Contractors

PROSPECTIVE
South District Council
East District Council
University Colleges (separate budgets)
Hospital (separate budgets)
Schools (separate budgets)
Private Schools
PSA (needs investigation)
Private Companies needing response based service
Housing Associations
>   Achme
>   Granville
>   Hapsberg
>   Harley
>   Stimpson

British Rail
General Public
Water Authority

To achieve market penetration a considerable effort is required. In the first year, up to 40% of a service manager's time is going to be taken in approaching customers internally and externally - through appointments and presentations etc.

This will drop off to 33% in future years but will always be a large part of the manager's duties. In that process we will be selling a full range of products including Building Maintenance, uPVC, specialist joinery products and highway maintenance, besides letting people know of our other services - refuse collection, parks and vehicle maintenance.

We need to know that once we have got the work, we can do the work. We therefore need to be able to attract employees and have a reliable stable of sub-contractors to offset peak workload. We will also need to present invoices for this work. We will need a group to manage the tendering and measurement of these works together with the payment and control of any sub-contractors. We already have in place Surveying and Estimating functions covering Building, Highways and uPVC production. As the number of customers expand the estimating and surveying need will grow. This will need to be regularly reviewed but the the starting point should be Quantity Surveying/Estimating with two subordinates.

The building industry has a poor image for quality and reliability. Although the industry is trying to do something about its image it has a long way to go. However, as a local authority, we should be able to capitalise on the advantages of being financially secure and of high quality. This would be added to if we could manage a quality assurance standard under BS 5750. This is a large investment but if we could demonstrate the added assurance this would give them, it could be helpful in selling the product. It should also be our goal to get our clients to include BS 5750 on a specification requirement.

Action 1: Provide resources to market the organisation

Target Date: Year 1

Action 2: Prepare promotional material

Target Date: December Year 1

Action 3: Investigate quality assurance to BS 5750

Target Date: Year 3

Besides trying to expand the business in areas where we already carry out work there are areas of specialist work that need investigating. These are listed below:-

1.   **Double glazed unit manufacture** - is a large capital investment and would need considerable research to justify it. However, it would fit in well with our present uPVC manufacturing unit, and also allow us to supply to other authorities manufacturing uPVC windows or using double glazed units.

Action: Investigate and report.

Target Date: End of Year 2

2.   **Central Heating Installation** -These contracts are generally let on a design specification basis. It is a fast turn round, low return operation. The amount of work available, assuming that we win the contract, only covers the six summer months. We would need a specialist gang for this with in-house design capability, which we do not have at the moment. We would need to

generate extra work during the rest of the year to make this worthwhile, which might be difficult.

Action : Investigate and report

Target Date: End of Year 3

3.   **Re-roofing -** We already have the expertise for this work but presently do not tender for it. We need to tender for this work in future.

Implementation Year 2 - ie tender for work.

4.   **Painting** - Same as re-roofing

Implementation Year 2 - ie tender for work.

5.   **Specialist Joinery Products** - We have an excellent woodmill and joinery shop producing one-off window frames, doors etc. We are already supplying South District Council and we have competed for some work at HDC and only narrowly lost.

It is clear that the larger joinery manufacturers are geared up to meet standard sizes and are not really interested in one-off work. However, from our simple research there seems a need for this.

We can operate fairly successfully with the present arrangements for small orders, and at the moment the housing repairs and maintenance contract gives the shop about ten months work with the other two months coming from work we get elsewhere within the authority plus some small outside contracts.We presently employ eight people within the unit.

This unit is at the limit of its physical capacity and it would not be possible to expand within the present space available. The only room for expansion would be through a shift system.

The other problem is that in the woodmill the machinery is ageing and an investment programme will be necessary. However, there does appear to be a ready market, so again a thorough investigation is necessary to see if development is justified.

Action: Investigate and report by mid Year 2

6.   **House Modernisation Schemes** - Investigate the potential of carrying out modernisation work.

Target Date: Mid Year 2

7.   **Rewiring Contracts** - Investigate the potential of expanding the electrical maintenance section by carrying out rewiring contracts.

Target Date: Mid Year 2

8.   **Sound proofing** - Investigate the potential of entering into this market.

Target Date: Mid Year 2

There is a considerable amount of research needed in the investigation of these ideas and at the present time there is no management time available. There is a clear need, if any of these ideas stand any chance of being implemented and marketed, for an extra managerial level to deal with the day to day problems of running the business.

Action: Set out organisation structure.

Target Date: September Year 1

14. STAFF/MANAGEMENT
14.1 General
All these plans will create major changes within people's working lives. They will be asking managers to take more responsibility for their actions and generally making them more accountable. This tends to create a reaction within people, basically because they are concerned about taking any action as it is easier to carry on in the existing patterns.

Clearly there is a need to define manager jobs to meet the new situation and to start with a completely clean sheet.

At the moment there are a number of barriers to flexibility through job titles and job descriptions. These need to be removed so that changes can be made relatively easily at any time.

It is clear at business centre manager level we need motivators and problem solvers with some technical expertise rather than solely technical managers. For this flexibility and accountability we need to prepare reasonable reward packages.

We need to achieve the right quality of flexible and accountable management through training and reward.

The fundamental principle for the organisation must be one of individual responsibility and accountability. To achieve this the people that manage must be given the tools to do the job.

The individual section manager cannot abdicate responsibility for the following:-

    1. Achieving a standard of work required by the client.

    2. Ensuring that the section has enough work to ensure continuity and that work is programmed and planned.

    3. Ensuring that the work is organised in an efficient manner and that all resources are used to their fullest.

    4. Ensuring that the personnel within the section comply with the bonus scheme in force.

    5. Ensuring that all work carried out is invoiced to the client, including variation orders and dayworks.

    6. Maintaining discipline procedures in accordance with the Council's policy, up to final warning stage.

7. Ensuring that all costs are accounted for.

8. Controlling the overall profitability of the section and making such reports as necessary.

9. Liaising with trade union representatives to solve bonus anomalies and formally recording such transactions.

10. Ensuring work is done in a safe and proper manner.

11. Checking work output for quantity and quality and formally reporting.

12. Attending out of hours emergencies as necessary and participating in any appropriate standby scheme.

13. Carrying out any other duties considered necessary for the well being of the section.

14.2 Structure Proposals

The structure must satisfy the following criteria:-

1. Make individual section managers responsible for their business centre.

2. Give people the resources to carry out the whole job and create team approach.

3. Produce more time for marketing, thinking and development of the business.

4. Allow for expansion of the business.

5. Create flexibility.

6. Give clients a service they require.

We would propose that achieving this should be carried out by the Building Services Manager, in conjunction with the Quantity Surveyor. To enable him to carry out this task there will have to be management support in the day to day running of the Building Section. To ensure that any expansion in tendering and quantity surveying workload is adequately covered, we would propose a staff of three initailly in the surveying section. These are important posts as they will maintain income through valuation and ensure that variation orders and contractual claims are dealt with.

These surveying/estimating posts will give us the ability to respond to our customers' contractual needs. As an indication of the tendering workload, details of the tenders submitted in the first three months of Year 1 were examined. We do not expect this workload to decrease. Managing these contracts when they are won, creates additional workload in terms of presenting valuations and negotiating variations to the contract. Again we expect this area of work to increase.

TENDERS SUBMITTED			
Period	Number	Value	Remarks
March, April May Year 1	81	£1,198,000	SoR Contract not included
Year 1	156	£1,207,000	SoR Contract not included
Prior Year 1	21	£56,000	
Prior Year 2	50	£55,000	
March, April, May Year 1	Split Builders work uPVC	£60,000 £1,138,000	
Year 1	Split Builders work uPVC	£317,000 £890,000	

Note this does not include the Building Schedule of Rates, which is worth £2,000,000

In addition to these changes we would propose to employ two new contract managers, one looking after the jobbing maintenance and the other looking after the small programmed works. They would have approximately equal turnover of £1.4 Million. These would be responsible for up to five agents but initially would look after three each. This will strengthen the management team with experienced managers, and allow more time for marketing. These managers would also be expected to control the administration of the section.

They would also be expected to stand in for agents when they are on holiday. We would thereby discard the stand-in supervisor arrangements that now pertain. It also allows for the reduction in administration personnel by one, as the contract managers take over this responsibility.

The supervisors are presently split on a trade basis. It is proposed that this is changed to an area or contract basis, thus giving full responsibility for any contract to one individual. It is also proposed that the salary be raised for these posts. This would consolidate the present overtime arrangements during the normal week, and only additional time would be paid for particular work. Managerial control at weekends would be on an agreed rota basis such that managerial paid overtime would be reduced from an average 500 hours per annum to 340 hours per annum per manager.

The administration personnel would be responsible for bonus calculation, work planning and general client contact. It is proposed that they would be paid as appropriate to recognise these responsibilities.

The estimated cost of these changes is £23,000 pa based on April Prior Year 1

It is proposed that the additional costs of this new structure are recovered through extra business and better use of resources.

Action: Introduce new organisation

Target Date: September Year 1

14.3 Training Requirements

Managerial Level - Business centre managers will need to manage their part of the business. This will involve training them so that they understand the information they are receiving, and what action they can take when problems arise. There will probably be a need to spend more time explaining what the new role of each manager is in terms of responsibility and authority. This will need to be done in the early statges of the organisation's launch.

Workforce - There is a need for the workforce as well as management to be flexible.

There is a shortage of building trade personnel at the moment generally and we are unable to recruit easily. There is a need therefore to consider apprenticeships and the retraining of more mature personnel.

A training programme needs to be established with clear objectives and costing.

Action: Produce a training and apprenticeship programme with implementation dates.

Target Date : Mid Year 2

14.4 Communications

Regular meetings are held with the supervisors to pass on and receive information.

Meetings are held on specific projects where the workforce are involved. Recent examples are the Building Maintenance Tender and the setting up of teams within the jobbing section.

The regular meetings with the supervisors will continue and as new ideas are conceived specific teams will be set up to examine them so that the full range of skills can be brought to bear.

All these meetings are minuted and passed to all present, together with copies for senior managers.

The workforce appear to be eager to meet the challenges and adjust to any changes necessary. They appear to want to beat the opposition and win. Involvement in the tendering process was met with enthusiasm, and constructive ideas, and they have tried team working with some success on tenancy changes.

Information is freely available and consultation will continue to take place regularly with new ideas and schemes. Consultation must be meaningful and directed towards needs.

Ideas will be encouraged from all levels and people will be encouraged to raise these ideas informally and formally. Teams will be established to examine these ideas as and when they arise.

Action: Continue meetings to solve problems as and when they arise.

Target Date: Ongoing

2. MARKET STRATEGY - BUILDING MAINTENANCE

ORGANISATION ATTITUDE

An organisation stays competitive by being perceived by its customers to be the best there is, not necessarily the cheapest; by taking the customer seriously and giving them what they want and need. The product comes before the money. Quality is achieved if everyone believes in it, if everyone contributes to it, and if everyone is always concerned first to improve their own quality of work. You get quality from quality people, trusted to work positively for the good of the whole organisation.

It will be necessary to drive out fear, break down barriers, encourage people to educate and develop themselves to work in teams to think for themselves, and to believe that everything can be improved forever.

What is marketing? - Markets do not buy products - customers do! Therefore any marketing strategy must cherish customers and not just marketing techniques. Any organisation hoping to get and retain customers must listen to them, treat them with courtesy and act on any suggestion or criticism.

1.   WHAT IS OUR BUSINESS?

1.1   What are we selling? -

A response based repair and maintenance service, able to maintain domestic housing stock.

An emergency repair service able to make safe most emergencies within domestic properties within 8 hours, 24 hours a day, 365 days per year.

A trade based building section able to cope with small works extensions.

Specialist joinery products.

1.2   What are our assets?

The staff, their experience and skills.

Being part of a local authority

Having a regular base workload

Buying power

2.   CUSTOMERS

2.1   What customers buy - Peace of mind at a reasonable rate - they do not necessarily go by specification and lower price. If it can be shown through mutual trust that the job that is being done is reasonable, then most customers are willing to pay. We must be seen as an honest and technically able concern. As an organisation we must give what the customers want and work closely with the customers to solve their problems. Customers do not want problems, they want solutions, and they are normally willing to pay for this.

2.2   Why customers buy - Customers buy because they have a need. They continue to buy because they trust the product will continue to give them the service they want. However, customers are not locked in; their needs change and the supplier is required to meet these changing needs.

In the area of building maintenance there is a need to recognise the changes taking place in the major customer (housing repair and maintenance), and follow their lead - particularly in their need to get close to the tenant and take more account of the tenants' needs. Whoever the client, there is a need to recognise and know where they are going.

2.3   How customers buy - Through a tendering process against a measured quantity, a specification and a time period. This can vary widely between schedule of rates, bill of quantity, lump sum or daywork contract over varying periods of time from 1 hour to 2 years.

2.4   When customers buy - At the end of contract periods or when internal and external pressures insist they do. Legislation (CCT)), TPAS report, change of personnel, change of policy. We need to be knowledgeable of what is going on around us and try and have the product ready for when the client needs it.

2.5   What customers expect - An expert response to their instructions so that buildings can be maintained well, causing the least inconvenience to their tenants at a reasonable cost. A reliable service that will do what it says when it says, and will solve problems with the customer as and when they arise. They will also expect to be charged for the work that is carried out.

2.6   Who are our customers -

Current:	
The Council	Leisure
Housing Repairs and Maintenance	DSO
Housing Estates	The County Council
Property	Local Health Authority
Architects	Local Housing Association
Engineering	The Housing Society
Environmental Health	General Public Contractors
Prospects:	
South District Council	Private Companies needing response based service
East District Council	
Colleges	Housing Associations: Achme, Granville, Hapsberg, Harley Stimpson
Hospitals	
Schools (separate budgets)	British Rail
Private Schools	General Public
Property Services Agency (investigate)	Water Authority

Presently over 90% of turnover is from the Council.

2.7   Where do we find the work - Local newspapers,trade journals, examination of committee minutes, personal contacts and Yellow Pages.

3.   MARKET MEASUREMENT
3.1   Size of market - Our present workload is £2.5M, an allowance has been made to expand this by one-third of a million pounds to an estimated turnover of £2.8M for Year 2.

We presently account for 67% of the Council's housing repairs and maintenance budget. The other 33% is spent with specialist contractors and other maintenance contractors because we do not have the skills or are unable to meet deadlines. Particular areas of specialist work are - re-roofing smaller percentage (probably in the order of 10%) from the capital programme although this is difficult to identify as uPVC replacement is mixed up in this workload, and is accounted for elsewhere. A major workload for the capital budget is fencing works.

We presently maintain 10,000 houses within the City. Taking housing associations and estimating that they have approximately 500 houses each, this would add another 3,000 houses and at least an additional £1M of maintenance work from this source within the City. Colleges, hospitals and other local authorities will have substantial repair and maintenance programmes and an additional £5M per annum market place within reasonable travelling distance would seem a conservative estimate.

3.2   Trends - The internal market within our Housing Department is under threat from legislation and the increased pressure on individuals to buy their houses.

The workload tends to be a reducing market rather than an expanding one. To maintain market share within the authority we would need to get into the specialist area such as re-roofing and central heating installation.

The other major trend that is apparent is a shortfall of skilled labour which means that a real control on the amount of work we can do is the amount of labour that we can attract and retain.

The greater involvement of individual tenants in the decision making process is going to affect our working arrangement in the future.

Tenants expect a fast response and that jobs should be carried out quickly - training will be required to improve planning and extend skills. It is becoming more important that the occupier is disrupted as little as possible. Therefore immediate response and fast turn round times are required. Wherever possible work should be completed in one day or at least on a continuous basis.

Looking on the positive side, we can offer an all embracing maintenance service and relieve housing management of the need to organise various trades. There is a niche for a reliable multi skilled organisation to meet housing management needs. This needs to be exploited with housing associations, district councils, hospitals and colleges where an all round service in a difficult market place may have major attractions.

3.3   Market Share - Internal market share approximately 66% of Housing R&M. Very small portions of other sections. External market share minor compared with market available.

There are large numbers of competitors ranging from large contracting organisations to "one man bands".

3.4   Seasonality - There are peaks and troughs of workload but work is available all year round. Troughs occur when budgets are being formulated and agreed.

4.   COMPETITIVE ANALYSIS

4.1   Competition - Mainly from the private sector although other local DLOs could be possible contenders (particulary South Council). The major players locally are J&K Plumbers, Inca, Mosells, Rolling & Willsens, and Brentwoods.

However, there are national companies who might be interested in our work in the future like Smiths and William Browns who already do work in similar circumstances for the PSA. These are just a few of the players locally and nationally.

Our competitors are normally used to doing minor works rather than repair and maintenance contracts to the level we operate at, but as market slow down does occur they might have to turn to this type of work to maintain turnover.

Few of these contractors are used to operating an emergency service on the same exacting basis that we do.

One of the other major advantages is a stores carrying a wide selection of goods at very reasonable prices. It is important that this advantage is maintained, and not passed to any competitor.

4.2   Competitive position - We dominate the Council R&M contract and we have extended our work to at least one housing association where we have carried out emergency works.

We now regularly supply wooden windows to South District Council.

There is work within the Council which we will need to attract more vigorously as well as outside markets.

It is important that we continue to sell a complete package and do not allow contracts to be broken down into small groups or trade based contracts. It is important that we compete against the major players in the market and not the small organisations.

It is imperative that we sell our ability to respond, and reliably, on all aspects of the work. It is also important that we note the customers wishes and provide speedy turn round on all operations.

4.3   Existing resource - We cover all the building trades and have sufficient resource to maintain our present market.

These resources are essentially split on a trade basis at the present time which means that multi trade jobs are difficult to organise and therefore often take several days to complete. There is a need to rearrange these resources so that they are more flexible in response and more team orientated.

To attract more resources from a limited labour market is difficult. We therefore need to rearrange the resources to achieve more production. The present bonus scheme is a blockage in this as it tends to stop progress, when maximum earnings have been achieved. A more flexible approach is needed. Our systems should not reduce our effectiveness.

Expansion can take place by the use of sub-contractors - our competitors can become our short term allies and be controlled accordingly.

Expansion to date has been limited and has only taken place through opportune meetings, rather than an all out attack on the market.

Therefore to expand a detailed plan of visiting and approaches must be made, and time must be put aside to achieve these goals.

We have said that turnover will increase by £300,000 during Year 2.

5.   MARKETING DECISIONS

5.1 Customer needs and preferences - Building maintenance needs to give a competent and speedy service. There is a problem in the definition of the customer, as contractually it is the Housing Department or the Housing Society, but in fact there is a hidden contract between ourselves and the tenant.

If the tenant is upset then the contractual client is upset. In most cases the tenant sees the property as a home and not as a housing unit. The contract with Housing would tend to give it this latter status. However it is clear that in fact this cannot be the case.

Due allowance must therefore be taken that we are entering someone's living space and that intrusion on this basis must be kept to the minimum.

Most customers want the job done on a continuous basis. They do not want delays where they are waiting for something to happen. Building works create mess. We therefore need to approach this problem and get our operations down to the absolute minimum. Our competitors are operating in this manner and getting rewarded for it. We must respond.

We must give a whole service to each individual tenant and estate manager and this should be a major selling point. Customers will keep coming back if they are satisfied. This will generate extra work - cost alone does not determine whether you get extra work.

The intention must be to work in unison with the client and not against them. We need them more than they need us.

5.2 Customer characteristics - The first point to note is that we have a number of customers - there is the client who is responsible for the property legally, and the tenant who lives within the property and has certain legal and moral rights and obligations.
The relationship between these two will be dictated by the attitude of the landlord and the policies.

It is the tenant's home. Therefore they want to be able to display a good appearance to the outside world. They do not like being disturbed. They want intrusion kept to a minimum. They are to a certain extent a captive market - but legislation is giving them more rights to break away. They want high quality work carried out courteously and tidily.

We are, however, perceived as not being able to meet these requirements.

5.3   Perception - We are Council employees, therefore we are no good, and it is the only job we could get. Do we believe this? - We cannot afford to. Our attitude has got to be that we do it better - and this can be demonstrated by a positive response to the client.

5.4   Business Bases -

1. A response based repair service.

2. A small works section capable of doing small building work, extensions, small buildings etc.

5.5   Business bases future - Need to look at specialist work re-roofing, central heating, guttering and lagging.

6.   MARKET POSITIONING
6.1   Purchase criteria -

a)	Can we do the job?	*Yes*
b)	Are we financially sound i.e. are we a good long term prospect?	*Yes*
c)	Are we competitive?	*Continuously tested and adjusted.*
d)	Do we keep our word?	*We are getting better but we can improve.*
e)	Do we do a good job?	*Yes*

6.2   Purchase preference - The customers need to be confident in the product and the producer. Need to know that they are not being over charged.

Our in-house customer still sees us as a part of the Council. This creates barriers, and uncertainty as to our role. We need to clearly identify as a separate organisation with specific goals and objectives. Therefore we need to project an identity linked to our functions and not just to the Council, which is a nebulous multi faceted organisation. People want clarity.

6.3   Perceptions of competitive products - We are seen as an arbitor in the market place - we do not outwardly embrace the profit motive. People tend to trust us, particularly other public sector bodies.

However, there are perceptions that we work inefficiently and to a poor standard. We need to dispel these rumours by actively projecting a positive image through uniforms, pleasant demeanour, clean vans, positive attitude and feeling good about ourselves, (training). Our best ambassador is the person who goes into the house. He/she needs to feel good about the organisation he/she works for. We must respect this investment.

6.4   New products - Need to investigate specialist working areas, eg Central heating teams, Re-roofing teams, Guttering, Specialist Joinery.

6.5   Existing service - Need to get people feeling good about the organisation. Need to identify with the organisation.

Need to break down barriers between "staff" and "manuals". Need to break hierarchical structure. Get rid of titles - people are not numbers or titles, they are individuals with their own requirements.

6.6   Customer perceptions - Everybody should see the customer as an individual to be treated with care and consideration. People are willing to pay more if they are treated properly.

7.   PRODUCT STRATEGY

7.1   Branding - We need to highlight our function and have a theme running through our organisation as a separate business. However, we need to take account of the fact that our name suggests quality and the word Council suggests financial soundness and fairness. We must overcome the downside of Council operations by better promotion of the organisation (DSO). There must be no identity crisis with our customers.

7.2   Service life cycle - Dependent upon contract cycles. It is important that we get better contract continuity. The Building Section presently relies for its viability on one large contract every two years. (Building R&M). This is extremely dangerous - we could lose everything at one go. To overcome this we need to reduce our dependence by winning other work and having a better flow through.

8.   PRICING STRATEGY

There is a need to sell quality and get specification adjusted to meet the service we offer whenever possible. This will help to exclude firms based solely on a profit motive.
Pricing willl have to reflect the situations as they arise. A more flexible approach is needed and must be adopted to suit each customer.

9.   PROMOTION STRATEGY

9.1   Targeting - Research must be carried out on potential customers to find out what they want, who to contact and how much work is involved.

There is no one now who has the specific responsibility for this. It is all achieved through ad hoc arrangements. Time needs to be created for this, probably at senior level - someone who can follow up any promises made. Obviously because time needs to be released for this, other staff will be needed to take up the extra workload. This will be approached through the business plan.

All our personnel should be aware and there should be a system where all employees are encouraged to bring in contacts.

9.2   Objective - To generate new business and to expand the turnover. £300,000 of work has been set as the target for Year 2 - a 12% increase.

9.3   Message - Substantial organisation; Professional approach and expertise; Diversity of services; Prompt and reliable; High quality; Good value; Long experience in public services; Care about the customer; Interested in the customer

9.4   Methods - Mail shots; Visits; Personal contact - all staff; Media response to tender requests; Respond quickly to any requests.

10.   AFTER SALES

10.1   Methods - Continue 9.4 - give advice and continue follow up visits.

10.2   After sales - During contract, request information on failures - and what is being done correctly; get a measure of customer satisfaction.

10.3   Service comparison - Need to get the measure of our competitors -

What are they doing?

What are they doing that clients like?

What are they doing that clients do not like?

As a result try and get specifications clear and precise in conjunction with client.

11.   ESTIMATED MARKET SHARE

Service features - We hold 67% of Housing R&M budget and about 10% of their capital spend budget.

Our credibility is improving but we need to be more flexible to customer demand. Generally we are recognised as giving a good service by the individual, but perceived as an amorphous mass generally because we have no clear identity other than being the "Council".

There is a high degree of knowledge within the section stemming from the supervision through to the tradespeople. They know the Council R&M section intimately and have good individual working relationships. The supervisors need reassurance that they can make changes and meet new clients without feeling the backlash of higher management. They need to be encouraged to take risks and see the benefits of such risk taking, and they need confidence in the organisation. This will reflect as confidence to our customers and generate confidence in the organisation.

We have a considerable purchasing power through our central purchasing unit. This should be utilised to the maximum with a further use of the system.

Our rate of return on assets is lower than our competition. Our better employment conditions should be promoted and sold more clearly so that we attract and retain more staff.

12. CUSTOMERS

The Council will remain our prime customer provided they retain their housing stock. However, this is a reducing market and we must look at other areas to replace this work.

The effect of Government legislation to reduce housing stock has been limited to date and with the authority's present commitment to retaining this stock, a reasonable workload has been maintained. The Government is on the offensive and although the changing of housing stock to private landlords will probably be resisted by the tenants, the possible increase in rent may make the right to buy situation more attractive.

We must have other avenues to maintain a reasonable workload.

13. IMPLEMENTATION

13.1 We need to research the market more and analyse these results more accurately.

13.2 We need to build up a prospect file and monitor this regularly.

13.3 We need to find resources to allow this to happen.

13.4 We need a training programme for people to understand the strategy and how they fit into it.

13.5 We need to get rid of old local authority attitudes and get the staff to see it as their business.

3. BUSINESS PLAN - PRINTING SERVICES

1. OVERVIEW

1.1   The Printing Section is responsible for providing an efficient and cost effective service to Council. Our prime business mission is to provide valued reprographic services to all clients and to generate revenue income for the DSO. This is our overriding goal towards which the section will strive.

1.2   Business History

Over the last decade the nature of the service provided has changed considerably. Ten years ago the Printing Section was part of the Treasurer's Department offering single colour and some multicoloured printing - all produced by conventional offset litho. All finishing was done by hand, all typesetting was sub-contracted and departments were still using stencil duplicators for short runs and committee minutes. The volume of business gave an annual turnover of around £35,000 and 5 staff were employed. Since that time we have progressed to high speed, high volume copiers with on-line finishing and a complete start to finish service, including graphic design, desktop publishing and a reasonably automated finishing section. Turnover has increased to £250,000 and 9 staff are employed. The section moved to the Chief Executive's Department 5 years ago and to the DSO last year.

1.3   Services Provided - The services currently offered by the section comprise:

Bulk photocopying with on line finishing	Perforating
2 colour photocopying up to A3	Folding
Desktop publishing	Booklet making
Graphic design	Binding
Single and multicolour printing	Guillotining
Numbering	Delivery service

In addition the Printing Section acts as agents in the provision of more specialist services, ie car park ticket printing, poster printing etc.

2. EXISTING CUSTOMERS

2.1   Our customers include:
The Council
The Festival Association
The Wildlife Trust
Family Planning Association
Other charities and public bodies

Our main customer will always be the Council with currently 85% of our turnover.

2.2   Our effectiveness is judged by the service we provide. Most customers are satisfied with quality, price and delivery, but our aim, by better monitoring, must be to keep all of our customers happy all of the time. The small minority of customers who were not satisfied with the quality of our service were given refunds when it was justified. Monitoring for delivery is by asking for a delivery date - most clients put "as soon as possible" on the order form, so we have no idea of the date required. If a deadline is missed a quick response is always initiated.

2.3   Improved communication with customers is necessary and essential - it not only keeps customers aware of any new developments and services, but gives the section a higher profile. Visiting clients on a regular basis, pre-warn of any unavoidable delays, monitoring meetings on large projects and hold an open day so that clients are informed about new services.

3. POTENTIAL CUSTOMERS

These include:
Other Authorities
Colleges
Schools
Housing Associations

4. BUSINESS ANALYSIS

4.1   The section has many strengths and they include:

(a)   **Committed Workforce** - The workforce is committed to the section and this is shown by the flexible attitude which enables changing priorities to be achieved and a responsive service is given. Regular staff meeting ensure information is shared, and everyone has a chance to contribute to the running of the section and get involved in the decision making process.

(b)   **Knowledge of the customer -** The very close contact with and intimate knowledge of the main customer's business means we can respond more effectively to them and anticipate future business needs. This represents a considerable advantage over outside competitors.

(c)   **Competitive Prices** - The prices charged are competitive for all services and in some areas are substantially lower than our competitors. A recent survey was carried out and the comparisons are listed below:

	Competitor A £	Competitor B £	Printing Section £
1000 - 3 colour A4 Heads	132 + VAT	210.79	113.12
500 - 2 colour A3 Posters	157	-	90
100 - 12 pp1 cover A5 Booklets	-	88	30

(d)   **Location** -The location is conveniently central for Council departments as speedy response times are essential to most areas of work and has the advantage of offering limited car park/pull up space.

(e)   **Sound Financial Base** - For many years the Printing Section has operated on a cost centre basis and the trading account has generally returned a small profit. The capital reserve fund which has been accrued by regular payment is available to finance investment as and when necessary. Overheads, with the exception of the internal accommodation recharge, are generally low.

4.2   The Section also has its weaknesses
(a)   **Old Equipment** - Whilst the section has invested recently in new equipment there remains a need to modernise two of the printing presses to enable higher productivity to be achieved.

Action - Renew the two presses. By acquiring machines of the same manufacturer, operating methods will be uniform, which in turn will achieve greater operator flexibility.

Target - within 3 years

(b)   Accommodation - The present accommodation, whilst probably adequate in size to meet present needs is poorly laid out and refurbished to a low standard.

Action - Although there is no room for expansion in our present location, better use of the existing space could be made. The first floor offices are to be altered and refurbished to incorporate a graphic design/DTP studio.

Target - Within 2 months

(c)   Poor Marketing - There is a clear need for the section to produce better information about the services it can provide. Many clients are currently unaware of the full range of services available. No real attempt has been made to market our services outside the council and external work has been generated by personal contact rather than through any planned or co-ordinated marketing drive.

Action - A vigorous marketing campaign beginning with the launch of the DSO and followed up by visits to potential clients with our marketing brochure.

Target - Launch of The DSO and ongoing

4.3   Opportunities for the section include:

(a)   Design Services - By bringing layout and design services in-house, work which at present is being contracted out by departments will be brought under our control. By offering a complete "start to finish" service, work will be generated not only for design but for printing as well.

Action - As in 4.2 (c)

Target - Ongoing

(b)   New Technology - Printing technology is in a state of rapid development. The opportunities afforded by new technology such as full colour laser copiers and more sophisticated DTP systems will need to be fully evaluated and exploited where possible. The Printing Section will need to keep abreast of and respond to new developments.

Actions - Reading trade magazines. Attending exhibitions and seminars

Target - Ongoing

(c)   Potential Customers - As stated in 4.2 (c) we have never marketed our services. There is a great opportunity to bring the services we can offer to the notice of new clients which will include colleges and other authorities.

Action - As 4.2.(c)

Target - ongoing

4.4   Threats to the section include:
(a)   Desktop publishing is a growth area and potentially very profitable, but if departments buy their own equipment not only could it be uneconomic for the authority

as a whole but could have a damaging effect on our profitability in this area.

Action - Publicise the fact that we have the right equipment with the necessary expertise to meet client requirements.

Target - ongoing

     (b)   **DSO Contracts -** If the DSO lose contracts then this will have a knock-on effect in all support services eg. lost printing of time sheets, job tickets etc.

Action - Ensure that we give the right support to front line services

Target - On going

     (c)   **Pricing** - The printing market locally is very competitive and expanding rapidly as the local economy grows and we will need to continuously review and monitor our prices against that of our competitors.

Action - Monitor the availability of printing for clients outside the council and establish our market niche in the short to long run single or two colour work. Retain and develop our market share in the area of business in which we operate by becoming more efficient with modern equipment and highly trained staff.

Target - ongoing

4. MARKET STRATEGY - PRINTING SERVICES

1. OUR BUSINESS

Our business is producing printed matter from photocopies to high quality four colour promotional literature:

- A desktop publishing system and a graphic designer
- Specialist finishing equipment

2. CUSTOMER ANALYSIS

2.1 What customers buy
- Expert advice on all printing matters
- Peace of mind at competitive prices and quality
- Advice on specialist printing

2.2 Why customers buy
- Preferred use of inhouse resources
- Greater contol over their jobs.
- Knowledge of the working of local government.

2.3 How the customers buy
- Internal customers - sending or bringing orders
- External customers - by telephone or personal contact

2.4 When the customers buy
All the year round, as and when they require printed matter.

2.5 What do customers expect
A quick response and value for money. Expert and professional advice.

2.6 Who are the customers
The Council, a housing association and various other customers.

3. MARKET MEASUREMENT

3.1 Size of Market - Potentially larger with the possibility of taking work in from other authorities, schools, housing associations and other public bodies.

3.2 Trends - Increasing more publicity material from the Council and an increase in the amount of colour work.

3.3 Market Share - Substantial but could be increased by better publicity of our services.

3.4 Seasonal - Not a problem since our services are required all year round.

4. COMPETITIVE ANALYSIS

4.1 Competitors - local printers; some offer good value for money but we can still equal or in most cases better their price.

4.2 Competitive position - We are in a strong position because of the depth of knowledge our customers require and the need to work within a budget.

4.3 Ability of New Entrants - There are local printers and franchise always coming into the market. Therefore our aim is to provide a service second to none.

4.4 Bargaining Power of Customers - Our customers have already been able to get competitive quotes for their printing and on rare occasions we have been unsuccessful.

4.5 Evaluation of Existing Resources - With the introduction of a new two colour printing press, extra capacity will be available which will be developed by selling our services outside the Council.

5. MARKETING DECISIONS

5.1 Customers Needs and Preferences - The customers need to be confident that we can supply the right goods at the right price and at the right time. Therefore, we must be professional in our approach towards them.

5.2 Purchase and Service Use - Customers are influenced by our ability to respond to their requests. Outside customers are influenced by a flexible approach, low cost and quick turnover.

5.3   Customer Characteristics - To be able to have total control over their jobs, especially highly confidential documents.

5.4   Business Base - Multi-niche offering black and white to full colour printing, photocopying, desk top publishing and graphic design.

6.   MARKETING POSITIONING

6.1   Purchase Criteria - Reliable prompt service and competitive prices.

6.2   Customer Preferences - The same as 6.1

6.3   Perceptions of Competitive Services - Plenty of competition, both small and large printers.

6.4   New Products - We have just introduced a graphic design service.

6.5   Perception of Existing Service - The present service is generally acceptable but there are some jobs where delivery and quality is below the standard set. Improvements are being made by better quality machinery and operator training.

6.6   Customers Perception - There are still some of our customers who think that we can only print black on white - the range of services will need promoting.

7.   SERVICE/PRODUCT STRATEGY

Need to highlight that we are part of the Council confirming reliability of service.

8.   PRINTING STRATEGY

Printing price is worked out for each job.Photocopying is charged on a cost per copy basis

9.   PROMOTION STRATEGY

9.1   Mailshots - prepare promotional literature and circulate to existing and potential customers.

9.2   Objective - To increase turnover by some 5% per annum particularly in the open market subject to the Local Government Goods and Services Act.

9.3   Message - Part of a large organisation - the Council. Good value for money, expert advice and reliable service.

10.   DISTRIBUTION AND AFTER SALES

10.1   Method - Follow up mailshots with personal contact. Find out what the customers want and give advice.

10.2   After Sales Service - Regular visits to customers to ensure their satisfaction and at the same time inform them of any new services available.

10.3   Service Comparisons - There are many printers both large and small within the area. We have to keep our service and prices as keen as possible. An advantage of being part of a large organisation is that we can bulk buy, therefore keeping material cost down. Disadvantage is the Goods and Services Act.

11.   ESTIMATED MARKET SHARE

11.1   Service Features - We are responsible for approximately 85% of all the printing required by the Council. It is hoped that this will expand a little through the installation of a two-colour press and extra DTP equipment.

11.2   Customers - The main customer will always be the Council but potential new customers could include schools, colleges, health authorities and housing associations. With careful marketing, it is possible to expand/generate up to 30% of our turnover from these new sources within the next 5 years.